WAR OF OUR FATHERS
Relics of the Pacific Battlefields

Photographs by Richard Marin

Foreword by Stephen E. Ambrose

Afterword by John McCain

CHARTWELL
BOOKS, INC.

For Allan Marshall Marin, Leonard Robert Marin, Gerhard D. Straus,

John A. Kelly, Stephen H. Ambrose, Leon Kogut, Irving Kogut, William A. Goldman,

John Sidney McCain Sr., John Sidney McCain Jr., Bansuke Itoh, and every veteran of WWII . . .

WITH REMEMBRANCE AND RESPECT

This edition published by
arrangement with and permission of
Marin Photography, Inc.

This edition published in 2001 by
CHARTWELL BOOKS
A division of Book Sales, Inc.
114 Northfield Avenue, Edison, NJ 08837

ISBN: 0-7858-1353-5

War of Our Fathers sponsored by
Eastman Kodak Company

Book art and layout by The Barnett Group/New York and Kato Kotaro Design Studio/Tokyo
Text typography design by Lynne Arany
Jacket design by Kevin McGuinness
Text by David Kogut

Printed and bound in China
01 02 03 MC 9 8 7 6 5 4 3 2 1
LFA

CONTENTS

FOREWORD

ONE WOULD SCARCELY KNOW it by looking at those of them left today, or by thinking about current Japanese-American relations, but oh my, how they hated each other. If possible more than the Russians or the French hated the Germans, and vice versa. From beginning to end, the Japanese-American war was waged with a barbarism and a racial hatred that was staggering in scope, savage almost beyond belief, and catastrophic in consequence.

Each side regarded the other as subhuman vermin. They called each other beasts, roaches, rats, monkeys and worse. Atrocities abounded, committed by individuals, by units, by entire armies, by governments. Quarter was neither asked nor given. It was a descent into hell.

Contemplate these photographs. The instruments of death and destruction are scattered across the Pacific, tucked away in islands that had no fame before the war and nothing but memories today, memories of screams, cries, weeping, mortification, blood wounds, death and more death.

At Iwo Jima, almost 80,000 marines invaded. There were more than 20,000 Japanese to defend the insignificant little island whose only claim to importance was where it was and that it had an airfield on it. The Japanese fought from caves, bunkers, tunnels, and they fought until dead. Virtually no Japanese were taken prisoner. The marines meanwhile suffered 5,885 dead and 17,272 wounded.

At Okinawa, 200,000 soldiers, sailors, and civilians died, including 12,281 Americans, including the commander, General Simon Buckner (whose father had been the Confederate General at Fort Donelson in the Civil War eighty years earlier).

The fighting in these Pacific islands, where the guns and fortifications seen today contrast so sharply with the peaceful scene of trees and sand, was of unimaginable ferocity. American POW's in Japanese hands were treated as slave laborers under conditions as dreadful as those in Hitler's camps. American POW's in German camps suffered a 4 percent death rate, as compared to a 27 percent death rate in Japanese camps. The United States bombed Japanese cities into oblivion, and with her submarines sank virtually all Japanese ships afloat, including men-of-war cargo ships, troop ships, tankers.

These catastrophes were caused by many factors, but the chief was the Japanese high command, which was criminal. The generals running the country would not quit, but instead were ready to fight to their last men—and women and children, come to that—who were being trained in the summer of 1945 to fight with sharpened bamboo sticks against invading Americans.

The generals were already disgraced. They had led their country into a war that they could not possibly win and carried it out with brutal disregard for the dictates of decency of the law of war. And they had fought stupidly. But they insisted on fighting on, to save their honor at the expense of their country.

Only the two atomic bombs forced them to surrender. Only thus was the worst war ever fought brought to its conclusion.

These pictures of that war, almost peaceful in appearance, speak to the horror of it all.

My father was there, a flight surgeon in the Navy stationed on Espereto Santo.

STEPHEN E. AMBROSE
Bay Saint Louis, Mississippi
July, 1999

WAR OF OUR FATHERS

Relics of the Pacific Battlefields

INTRODUCTION

WE GREW UP SURROUNDED by heroes; real ones, with medals, aching wounds, and dark tales of valor.

We learned in snippets of their struggle and sacrifices. In our childhoods, we would overhear a stray comment, see a pale line or circle on abdomen or arm; startle to a cry erupting from a nightmare marring Dad's Sunday afternoon nap.

And we wondered. What Hell was this? Where had he been? What had they done? What had been done to them?

We wondered, too, that dark question of manhood: Could I do it? Could I expose myself to this terror? Would I stumble bravely onward through the fog of war? Could I let myself be so humbled, so humiliated—what does it really mean to volunteer to serve, knowing full well that a pea-sized piece of lead could reduce me to oblivion?

Some have said our fathers did not know what they were getting into; they answered the call for men at arms blindly, propelled by passion more than reason. Some have called the era encompassing World War II and the years leading up to it "naive," or even "innocent."

Bullshit!

As we grew, we learned that they knew, most of them knew: The war of our fathers was not the war of John Wayne. There was no glory on the sands of Iwo Jima, only the redemptive state of grace called survival.

Our fathers went to a war they waged with bitterness, rage, and a sense of betrayal. They went to war reluctant, angry, determined but maybe not too much so. When a new Asian war ripped through the ranks of our generation, we learned—our fathers sometimes told us calmly, in voices even with compassion—of men who would blow off a toe to escape combat duty, of trunk lids dropped on knuckles, and of envy and prayer for the "million-dollar wound"—injury not bad enough for permanent crippling, but serious enough to send you permanently *hors de combat*.

We learned, as we grew up, that the war of our fathers was fought by men—and some women—all of whom had blistered in the Great Depression.

Their war flowed seamlessly in a line of time from the days of "Parlor Pinks" and persecution of the Scottsboro Boys; of a "radio priest" oozing hatred; of a handful of idle and gussied rich flaunting wealth and flouting the tenets of generosity while a quarter of a nation went starving.

They went to war still singed by the sight of people collapsing from hunger. Seared by visions of the dignity of labor reduced to the mockery of idleness.

They went to war with no grand or flag-waving illusions to blind them. They were risking their lives by feeding themselves into a giant, impersonal, and macerating maw to preserve democracy; in Churchill's words, "the worst form of government except all those other forms that have been tried."

They knew, full well, they were submitting

themselves to a merciless system profiting handsomely on their valor: Shortly before the war, elevated train tracks were stripped from New York's Sixth Avenue. The scrap steel was sold to an already-aggressive Imperial Japan. Laborers at the demolition ruefully predicted, "We'll buy it back at twenty-one bucks a month"—the base pay of an Army private.

They knew where the steel was going. And they knew its eventual target. Their foresight was soon borne out. The Sixth Avenue "El" returned—right on schedule, arriving at stations in the infernos of beaches and jungles with unpronounceable names and battles of unspeakable ferocity.

They went because they had to. They went because the job needed doing. The purpose was clear and the alternatives few. They went reluctantly, caustically; and not even all of them—some evaded, some refused, some sought "safe" duty, and some dissolved in the face of battle. Those who went rooted themselves in something identifiably and persistently American, the feeling that in them was vouchsafed "the last best hope" of humanity on Earth.

For some of us, there was a difference, a hesitation. We had no pictures of Dad at the Eiffel Tower in the autumn of 1944; nor could we revisit with our fathers the pub in East Anglia where they whiled away the hours between missions; neither could we seek out for him the family he had befriended when he was on garrison duty in Italy.

The war of *our* fathers was waged at the end of the Earth. We could not visit this place—even today. It was war on a dot at the end of a string of specks in the mapmakers' blue Pacific. Who had heard of Attu? Eniwetok (Any-wee-tok)? Or the Marshalls, Gilberts, or Saipan, or its junior twin, Tinian?

Who had heard of Tinian? Good Lord! We never heard of Tinian, yet how many places are more important in the annals of recorded time than Tinian?

If Cape Canaveral is revered, then Tinian is hallowed. It, too, was a launch pad—for the *Enola Gay* and *Bock's Car*. From its runways, nuclear destruction took wing.

For better or ill, Tinian is a hallowed place.

So, too, then is Unimak—American soil invaded by the Empire of Japan. And so, too, is Okinawa, where 12,281 Americans died in two months, in preparation for the holocaust of an invasion of Japan's "home islands."

And we must observe, too, the sanctity of Tarawa, "Bloody Tarawa," where more than 3,000 fell to "secure" an island half the size of New York's Central Park.

Weep and pray for the fallen on the infernally black sands of Iwo Jima—taken to provide fighter plane bases for the bombers on Saipan and Tinian. Light candles if you will, for the reluctant heroism of them all.

If Gettysburg is hallowed ground, then surely the Divine rests in these places, too, to give meaning to the war of our fathers; our fathers, whom we know all too well to be ordinary men.

At the peak of their power, the Ancient Romans boasted of the Mediterranean as *mare nostrum,* "our sea." In truth, it was. The Caesars imposed the *Pax Romana* on the known world.

Yet this pales beside the epic reaches of Japan's empire at its zenith. A fifth of the Earth was under the sword of the emperor; very nearly, the world's greatest ocean was their *mare nostrum.* They called their regnum the Greater East Asia Co-Prosperity Sphere.

The power of the Chrysanthemum Throne seemed invincible as 1942 glided towards a cautious America and an already-weary Great Britain. Japan's forces seemed able to spring upon corners of the world simultaneously, from China and the edges of the Indian subcontinent to Australia, Indochina (later, Vietnam, Cambodia, Laos), Alaska, and the Hawaiian archipelago. Troops stormed the Philippines; made a surprise attack on Singapore, through "impregnable" jungle; overwhelmed Hong Kong and swept into Burma.

And—instructed by successes in the canvassed pages of Japanese military history—the empire executed a daring, successful, and flawless sneak attack on the American fleet at Pearl Harbor.

Ironically, if one asks a Japanese person today about December 7, 1941, a "date that will live in infamy" and the memory of astute schoolchildren, the only likely rejoinder is a blank look. The date in Japan,

for the beginning of what is now called "The Disaster," is December 8—a Monday.

The beginnings of "Pearl Harbor," however, long preceded the establishment of the International Date Line. Japan had been long ill-served by a nationalistic and parochial elite.

For nearly three centuries, the Tokugawa Shogunate (ruling war lords) kept Japan sealed from the wider world. The only foreigners (literally, in Japanese, *gai-jin,* "foreign" or "strange ones") were confined to small trading centers.

When the American "black ships," eructing fire and vapor like harbinger comets, arrived off Japan's shores in 1853, modernity began with a tumult. The myth of Japanese racial and cultural "purity" and superiority struck dissonances as it clanged against the technology and "sophistication" of the West.

Japan would not be left behind again. The people studied, learned, and grew their nation. Respect for the emperor—waning under the shoguns—was restored and embellished as a unifying force, a divine force.

Already alarmed, the American secretary of state John Hay in 1899 proclaimed the "Open Door" policy, which became a cornerstone of this country's foreign relations. The East was to be a marketplace for all, a freewheeling nexus of commerce.

The policy seemed sensible to an America suckled on the West's historic fascination with Cathay, the land of Marco Polo, China. America was "discovered" by Columbus's ostensible quest for the shortest route to the land of ruby-cored mountains.

From the earliest days of the republic, Salem ships sailed for the Orient. Lovely teak-crafted clippers like the *Cutty Sark* sped tea to the New World. In Hay's own lifetime, the intrepid defied the ice floes in search of a Northwest Passage, that East might more quickly meet West.

A ripening and increasingly fearsome Japan saw the East as the domain of Asians. Prompted by victories over the Russians in 1905, by its unassailed and savage dominion over Korea, and its position among the victorious World War I Allies, Japan's power grew unchallenged. The empire needed markets, raw materials, and sheer space—the Germans called it a need for *lebensraum*—to expand beyond a constrained, resource-poor home archipelago.

Willing to use assassination to accelerate their ascent, the militarists staged the 1931 "Manchurian Incident" and seized power there. China was the ultimate prize. In 1937, Beijing and other cities were seized. The next year, Japanese troops ran riot in the "Rape of Nanking." The world uttered no more protest than it had a year earlier, at the destruction of Guernica. Modern warfare dawned upon an unprepared world.

Yet the world had been warned. Even before Cassandra-like tocsins of Hitler's ascent were scorned, the early seers of Japan's bellicosity were already being met with punishment. That was the fate of America's most famous "Prophet Without Honor."

The exact charges were couched in the legalese and officious ink-and-seals of military code, but history has harshly judged the officers court-martialing a fellow general, Billy Mitchell.

A hero of World War I aviation, Mitchell made a spectacle of sinking captured German battleships, demonstrating the vulnerability of dreadnoughts to even the meager airpower of old spindly biplanes and crudely aimed bombs. As Assistant Chief of the U.S. Air Service, he strongly advocated a separate air force, and pushed for newer and safer planes. He was a visionary when it came to air power, and in 1925, openly critical of the unpreparedness in the Pacific, he warned that "Japan may unleash a war in the Pacific. She could attack America by striking first at Hawaii, some fine Sunday morning."

His tireless promotion of the Air Service pitted him against the status quo preferred by the Navy brass and the special interests in the government, and he was rewarded with a demotion and a transfer. Taking his case to the press, he charged officials responsible for a recent crash with "Incompetence, criminal negligence, and almost treasonable administration of the national defense." He expected to be court martialed, and was and used his 1925 trial to further argue his position.

At his trial, Mitchell foresaw that war in the Pacific would be waged from land base to land base, mounted by armies under cover of superior air forces. It is possible that even then someone produced the phrase that would ring throughout the Pacific War: "island hopping." It means bypassing enemy garrisons, of as many as 100,000 men, to let them wither without hope of resupply or evacuation.

Some may have taken note of Mitchell's premature wisdom, but not before he was convicted and drummed from his beloved corps. But the vote was not unanimous. No one is certain but most—then and now—believe the sole exonerating ballot was cast by a valiant friend of Billy Mitchell, a vainglorious student of history and the mistakes of himself and others, an officer recently promoted to major general through his politically connected mother's intervention: Douglas MacArthur.

Beribboned for his well-witnessed and genuine valor under fire in France in World War I, MacArthur commanded the garrison in the Philippines from 1922 to 1930. In 1941 he was back in the islands as head of the U.S. military mission, and as a signal to the Japanese, Roosevelt named him Commander-in-Chief Far East. When the Japanese forces struck, it was less, much less, than his finest hour.

The same day (but not date, due to the date line) as Pearl Harbor, MacArthur was aware of the attack, but not that other Japanese attacks were already underway throughout the islands. His air force wanted to attack the Japanese fields in Formosa, which could be reached by their B-17 bombers, but he was reluctant to be the one to make the first offensive strike of the war. His bombers and fighters took to the skies, circled aimlessly for a while, and returned for lunch. That was when the Japanese attacked, bombing and strafing the row upon row of parked planes. The Japanese lost only seven fighters and no bombers, having shot down twenty-five fighters and destroyed seventy bombers and fighters on the ground.

The invasion started shortly after, with the main body of 43,000 Japanese landing on the Lingayen Gulf on December 22. The invading forces—in some places weaker than his own—consolidated and exploited the Allies' retreat to pockets on the fortress of Corregidor and in the Bataan Peninsula.

By New Year's Eve, it was a stand-off, with both sides dug in for a siege. The Japanese were able to re-supply while the Americans and Filipinos could not, and malnutrition joined the enemy. MacArthur, thought too valuable to be abandoned to enemy capture, was ordered to depart his embattled headquarters on Corregidor by President Roosevelt. On March 12, the general and his entourage were spirited from the fortress by PT boats. The war never left the island for its duration.

The Prussian general von Clausewitz dictated that the objective in war is to destroy the enemy's army. True enough, and on its face, eminently logical.

Von Clausewitz, however, wrote of an era of professional armies obsessed with perfecting flanking maneuvers. He preceded the era of total war.

More than politics or diplomacy by another

means, war in our century has become a kind of grisly economic contest—two or more nations in a cataclysmic collision of resources; peoples laying waste to one another's homes and populations until the exhausted surrender.

Some in Japan knew and understood. The attack on Pearl Harbor was a tactic of another century: It only sought to destroy an enemy's striking arm. It did not lay waste his will or means.

Ironically, it was the architect of the attack, Adm. Isoroku Yamamoto, who best perceived the ultimate impossibility of Japan succeeding in total war. A former attaché in Washington, he grasped America; had seen the vastness of its reaches and its potency even in slumber. He promised the Japanese war planners six months of victories in which they could establish a defensive perimeter that would allow the Empire to control seas from the mid-Pacific islands to the East Indies. Without the Pacific Fleet, the Americans would eventually be worn down to a negotiated peace.

When the mission commanders returned to their carriers, flush from the attack, they recommended additional strikes at Pearl Harbor. They were overruled by admirals satisfied that they had executed their plans and followed their orders.

Thus were spared the fuel reserves, repair shops, and submarine pens at America's vital mid-Pacific station. A later raid—or a more strategic first attack—might have extended the war by a year, or forced a negotiated peace.

Instead, an aroused though unprepared nation roared its rage and defiance.

A nation stirred under the paternal hand of a President in office for nearly nine years. The youth of the nation streamed into recruiting stations; unschooled and unprepared, America returned to war.

A French journalist interned in Tokyo for the duration of the conflict wrote that before the end of 1942, Japan's leadership knew their cause was essentially lost. The words gave a chilling and stunning effect when recounted to veterans.

Not only did three full years of apocalyptic slaughter lie ahead, but at times the Allied cause seemed in grievous doubt.

To the International Date Line and sometimes beyond, Japanese forces roamed seemingly at will: Dutch Harbor, Alaska, was bombed. Explosives rained on Darwin, Australia. Japanese submarines surfaced off California to impudently lob shells.

Japanese forces strode over most of New Guinea, which sits like a mantle over Australia's populous eastern coast. From air bases in the Solomon Islands, guarding the sea lanes to the Island Continent, they threatened to strangle a vital ally.

On May 6, with the final surrender in the Philippines, there were no Allied forces left in the Northern Hemisphere of the Pacific between Hawaii and Ceylon. Admiral Yamamoto had delivered his six months.

Battles at sea were sometimes claimed as

triumphs, and in truth the imperial advance was halted at Midway and near the Coral Sea in June 1942. But the victories were more in the tradition of Pyrrhus than David Farragut. The Japanese savaging of the U.S. Navy off Savo Island in August was its worst trouncing in a fair fight since John Paul Jones.

Hampered by defective torpedoes—a problem not corrected until late 1943—the American submarine fleet suffered frightening losses. A tiny service which came to play a mammoth role in the strangling of Japan's supply lines, the undersea mariners paid the war's highest price among all the Allies's forces. One in ten is "still on patrol."

With whatever forces they could muster, the Allies—led by Americans and Australians—fought back. No, they clawed back.

The U.S. forces, under Adm. Chester Nimitz, would lead a two-pronged advance, with MacArthur advancing across the southwest Pacific towards the Philippines, while Nimitz would fight his way West across the central Pacific. The Allied plan was to concentrate first on the Solomons, on to the Gilbert Islands, then to the Marshalls, followed by the Eastern Carolines and the Marianas.

In New Guinea, the Diggers—Australians—carved a 4,000-step staircase in the Owen Stanley Mountains—and focused the world's attention on a hellacious path, soused in blood and bodies—the Kokoda Trail.

Americans waded into the Solomon Islands, spearheaded by marines, supported by the air and naval units that could be spared or that had survived. From August 1942 to February 1943, Liberty held her breath. The islands had to be taken to keep Australia secure. The one with the major airstrip was most important: Guadalcanal.

It was on Guadalcanal that the name "Bloody Ridge" passed onto a scroll begun at Lexington. It was also probably on Guadalcanal that stranded, obdurate marines began using the Chinese expression for "pull together" and made it a battle cry: "Gung ho."

From the west, British, Chinese, and Indian troops pressed the borders of the empire. Burma refused to surrender. Supplies were trucked by the legendary Burma Road to China or flown "over the Hump" of the Himalayas to a Chinese army supported by American advisors.

Total war with Japan meant crippling the enemy's industrial base. Short of invasion, that was the task of bombers—especially the new, long-range, heavy-duty B-29s. Plans were made for the B-29s to fly across the East China Sea and southern Sea of Japan and pummel factories, piers, fuel tanks, and rail lines.

China remained chaotic, and the logistics of supplying bases there proved insurmountable. The planners' arrows began to focus on the Marianas—Saipan, Tinian, and Guam are the largest.

In late 1942 or early 1943, however, the Marianas were far beyond Allied reach; the Japanese would have to be beaten back across the Pacific.

Submarines began unrestricted warfare against Japan.

Under MacArthur's direction, the defending forces were split in stifling Japan's supply lines. Tankers, supply ships, even capital warships were unremittingly sent to the bottom. Maintaining the huge defensive perimeter they had created necessitated supplying it, and as the Allies made their slow inroads, the Japanese began to feel the pinch.

Confounded at first by superior Japanese aircraft and the skill of imperial pilots hardened by battle in China, American aviators gradually gained experience, acumen, and equipment. At the same time, the Japanese were facing a dwindling number of experienced carrier pilots.

The tactics of amphibious warfare still needed honing. Mindful of the wisdom of Billy Mitchell, MacArthur sought air cover for each leg of the island-hopping advance. The Gilbert Islands were next.

The first amphibious battle, perhaps the worst battle, was around Tarawa in November, 1943. The marines ignored the advice of native Chamorros and attacked the main island of Tarawa Atoll—a coral hummock called Betio—at low tide. The shock troops had to wade, swim, stumble, and bleed 700 yards to the beach under withering fire.

"Bloody Tarawa"—really Betio, just half a square mile—cost the American forces 985 dead; 3,300 casualties in all. The Japanese lost 4,700 men, with only 17 combat soldiers taken alive.

"Body counts" were not invented in Vietnam.

Casualty ratios of nearly 1:1 brought the marines under congressional scrutiny.

Planning improved but the fighting remained bloody and fierce, with Japanese troops fighting to the death. Kwajalein and Eniwetok in the Marshalls were the next "stops" in the eastward advance. Each exacted a price on the roll to the Marianas in January 1944. In the first, all but 130 of 8,000 Japanese died, in the second, there were no survivors among the 2,200 troops. American losses in each were about 400.

Saipan, the largest island—only three times the size of Manhattan—was invaded just nine days after D-Day. Casualties are hard and loathsome to compare, but marines who led the assault boast their losses were worse than Omaha Beach. While "mopping up" continued—a term resented by Army troops who had the dirty task of hunting down snipers and pockets of resistance—one-by-one-work began immediately on what was to become Isley Field. Amid sniper fire, Army Air Corps troops began cutting cane and readying for the bombers.

Hideki Tojo, the Japanese mastermind of this war, resigned as Prime Minister. The safety of the home islands could no longer be assured. On November 24, 1944, B-29s flew from Saipan to Tokyo. The raids—including a March 1945 night of terror that claimed more lives than either atomic bomb—continued unabated until the surrender.

Just over a month before, on October 20, 1944, MacArthur waded ashore at Leyte—actually, several times, for the benefit of photographers. In the rush of what would come to be called "visuals," he got off what would come to be called a "sound bite": "People of the Philippines, I have returned."

Ordinary GI's were not thrilled to help MacArthur make good on his 1942 promise. Manila gave them their only experience in the kind of house-to-house fighting familiar in the European theater of operations. And MacArthur spent nine months clearing all the major Philippines islands of Japanese troop concentrations—his only deviation from the strategy of bypassing enemy garrisons when possible.

Though MacArthur was already ashore at Leyte, the Japanese were determined not to allow the empire to be cleaved in two: They sent the balance of their navy to isolate the landing force and deprive it of replacements and resupply.

Between October 23 and October 25, a series of six naval engagements broke the spine of the imperial force and chilled the world with an unspeakable tactic. The Battle of Leyte Gulf is recorded as the greatest encounter of its kind in history. World War I's Jutland involved about 250 ships. There were more than 280 at Leyte, with 187,000 sailors and hundreds of airplanes.

A navy that began the war by sinking two of Britain's proudest capital ships in one day was settling on the bottom. A total of twenty-eight ships—4 carriers, 3 battleships, 10 cruisers, and 9 destroyers—were sunk in the engagement.

Volunteer fliers, however, brought a new,

desperate tactic into the war. Deliberately crashing their planes into their targets, they were dubbed the *kamikaze,* after the "divine wind" that destroyed a Mongol invasion fleet in 1215.

As pressure on the home islands—by submarines, bombers, and the threat of invasion—mounted, resistance became all the more determined.

Allied bombers returning to Saipan and Tinian needed a way station in the trackless Pacific. Also, their fighter planes, lacking the range of the lumbering bombers, could not fly escort over Tokyo.

Draw a straight line from Saipan to Tokyo and midway it will pass close to Iwo Jima. Iwo was invaded on February 19, 1945. It was the crucible of the U.S. Marine Corps, its time on the cross. All the more so because the globe-and-anchor was being worn by draftees; through most of the war the Corps' billets were barred to conscripts. The draftees were dubbed "handcuffed volunteers."

The marines suffered 5,885 dead and 17,272 wounded. There were 21,000 Japanese troops on the island. All but 200 died. Congress was silent on casualty ratios this time: Iwo had to be taken. This time there were no alternatives.

Nor was there anything like the battle fought by John Wayne. The black sands of Iwo Jima bear little resemblance to the balmy precincts of Catalina Island, where the movie was filmed. Even Joe Rosenthal's celebrated photograph of the flag-raising on Mount Suribachi is mute testimony to the awfulness of the fighting. Three of the six men in the picture died in the battle.

Gallantry's only reward was the call for renewed sacrifice. In anticipation of the invasion of Japan, the garrison on Okinawa would have to be neutralized. Note the dates well: The battle was fought from April to June 1945. Japan fought on unabated after Germany surrendered and Italy had already gone over to the Allied camp.

In the space of that campaign 200,000 human beings lost their lives. Of them 12,281 were American, including the invasion commander, Gen. Simon Buckner. In one two-day offensive alone, *kamikazes* and bombers killed 628 sailors.

There is a saying that anyone will crack under the strain of combat; it's only a matter of when. Okinawa, for many, was "when." By the end of May, the forces assaulting Okinawa could count more than 14,000 "neuro-psychiatric" cases among their ranks. If there were ever illusions of glory, they had been wrung from a battle-weary country.

The imperial navy was gone, and the army was retreating throughout the former empire without direction or supply. At home, the bombing campaigns of Curtis LeMay reduced the five major cities of Japan to rubble. Over three million were homeless in Tokyo alone. By mid-summer up to 800 bombers were attacking at a time, and the Japanese air defense was virtually destroyed. Invasion plans were being drawn up by the army and navy.

While the Japanese believed there were two alternatives to end the war: Invasion or negotiated peace, President Harry S. Truman weighed the cost of invasion against the third alternative the Allies possessed.

On August 6, the *Enola Gay* (named for its pilot's mother) roared off the runway at North Field on Tinian. The atomic age began and the war was soon to end.

Illness, wounds, and trackless scars would start to heal. For some, there would never again be a time when they felt so active, so vital, so involved and important as in the three-year span of America's Pacific War.

For most, the job was done and a homecoming was to be attended to. The terrors were to be sealed off, forgotten, left to wither as time isolated them like some bypassed Japanese garrison.

This was the war of our fathers.

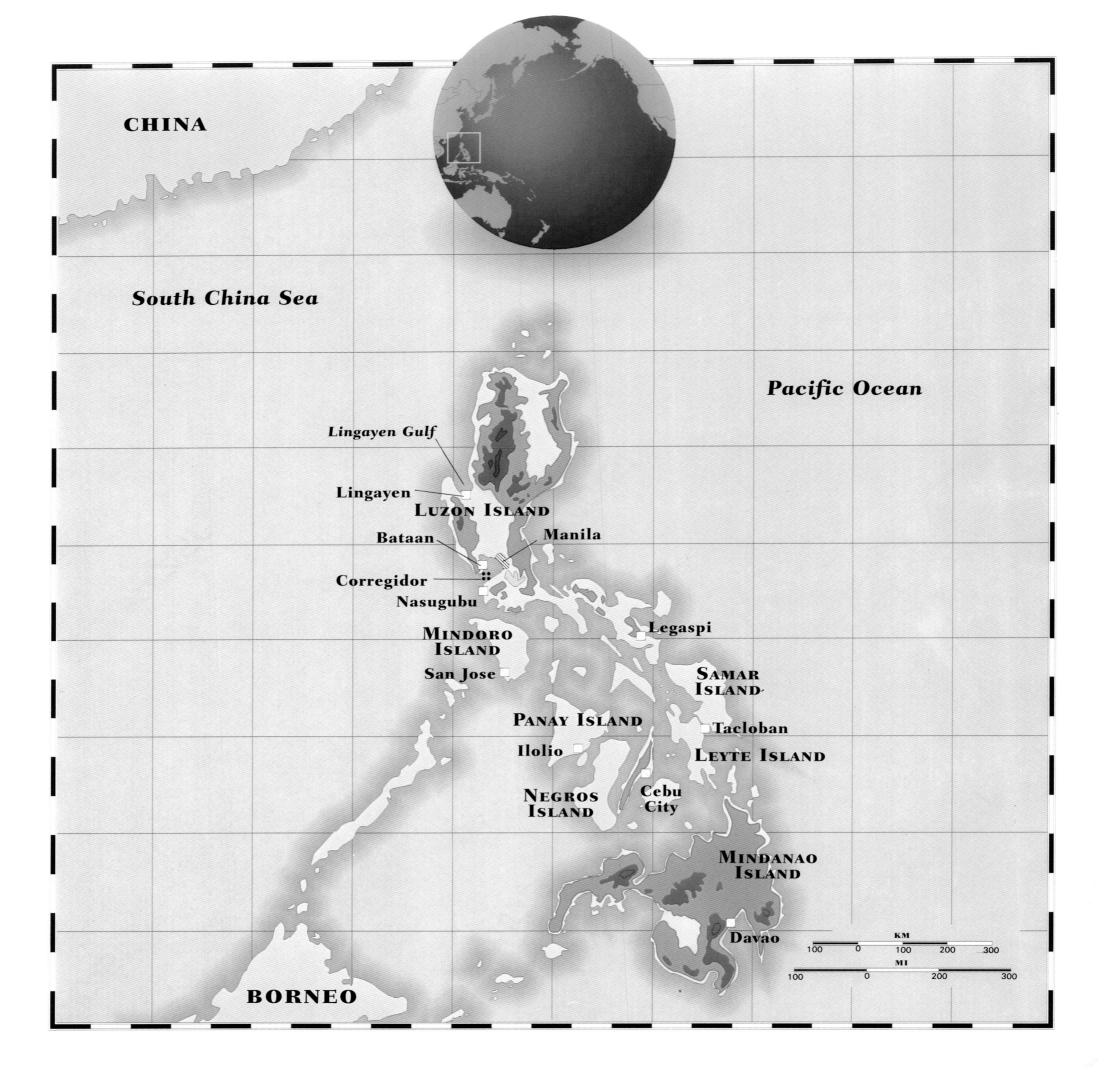

CHINA

South China Sea

Pacific Ocean

Lingayen Gulf

Lingayen

LUZON ISLAND

Bataan

Manila

Corregidor

Nasugubu

MINDORO
ISLAND

Legaspi

San Jose

SAMAR
ISLAND

PANAY ISLAND

Tacloban

Ilolio

LEYTE ISLAND

NEGROS
ISLAND

Cebu
City

MINDANAO
ISLAND

Davao

KM

100   0   100   200   300

MI

100   0   200   300

BORNEO

THE BATTLES: A six-month siege begins after the attack on Pearl Harbor and ends with 76,000 American and Filipino prisoners on the Bataan Death March and the fall of Corregidor a month later. THE GENERAL: Douglas MacArthur, possessed of an abiding love of the islands, where he had first come under fire, where his father had been military governor. THE VOW: "I shall return." THE LANDING: At Leyte, October 20, 1944. FIGHTING: Until June 1945. THE COST: An estimated 70,000 Japanese dead and nearly 16,000 Americans.

BATTERY SMITH/AMERICAN
Corregidor Island
Disabled 1942

THERE WERE ACTUALLY TWO BATTLES in the Philippines, or three, including one of the largest confrontations at sea in history. Named for Spanish royalty, scene of Spanish—and American and Japanese—ignominy, these islands and their graceful people have known little peace in this century.

Arthur MacArthur, Jr., a general and a civil war hero, became military governor of the islands in 1900 after Gridley and Admiral Dewey demolished the Spanish fleet in Manila Harbor. Forty years later, his son Douglas headed the U.S. military mission, charged with preparing the by then self-governing commonwealth for independence.

Within hours of Pearl Harbor, Japanese planes from Formosa attacked, finding virtually all of the American planes on the ground. With air support virtually eliminated, the island prepared for invasion. Of the 130,000 troops, only 20,000 were Americans up to "normal standard," the balance were Filipino units, many still in training and not fully equipped.

The Japanese landings quickly took airbases in the north, and the main invasion force of 43,000 landed at the Lingayen Gulf, but further north than the defenders expected, and they swept south with little resistance.

Under MacArthur's direction, the defending forces were split in two: The "Battling Bastards of Bataan" mounted a heroic defense of that peninsula, while their commander kept his headquarters at Corregidor, in the 1,400-foot Malinta Tunnel. He was given the sobriquet "Dugout Doug." Adding to this reputation was the order, obeyed on March 12, 1942, for MacArthur and his family to evacuate Corregidor. Reaching Australia, he uttered his famous vow, "I shall return." For his troops, the emotion was mixed.

Bataan fell on April 9, with about 76,000 troops taken prisoner.

From hours after the attack on Pearl Harbor until the surrender in Tokyo Bay, war never left the Philippines. Americans and Filipinos fought as partisans or returned in reconquest.

◊ ◊ ◊

There would be no reinforcements for the defenders. The promised convoy with troops and supplies had been diverted to Australia.

What followed was one of the most notorious episodes of the Pacific War.

There is a saying that there are survivors to every massacre, and the Bataan Death March was no exception. In the words of one observer, Japanese soldiers considered those who surrendered "damaged goods." Some 350 or more officers of the Ninety-first Division were summarily executed by sword and bayonet. Men were killed for asking for water. Trucks ran down prisoners on the march; an officer was beheaded for possessing currency. An estimated 600 Americans and untold thousands of their Filipino allies perished.

It would be a long campaign back to Bataan. It was not until October 20, 1944, that Army troops landed in Leyte to reconquer the islands and MacArthur "returned." (Word quickly spread through the ranks of the repeated "takes" of MacArthur's celebrated wade-in through the surf. Ever public-relations-wise, MacArthur named the transport he used throughout the war "Bataan.")

The fight for the Philippines—justifiable, perhaps, given their strategic importance—was to continue for the duration of the war. Manila was not liberated until March 1945 and Luzon not until June—*after* Okinawa was declared secure. The estimated casualty toll was 70,000 Japanese and nearly 16,000 Americans. Strategists and "dogfaces" alike continue to question the need to secure all of the major Philippine islands. It was the only major deviation from successful island-hopping assaults.

At the outset of the campaign to return to the Philippines, however, Japan's Navy mustered what came to be its last gasp. The Battle of Leyte Gulf was the largest in history, involving 280 ships and 187,000 men on both sides. It finished the Japanese naval air arm and sent one-fourth of Japan's Navy to the bottom—three battlewagons, six heavy cruisers, and four carriers among them—a total of twenty-eight ships, to America's six.

FORT BONIFACIO/AMERICAN MILITARY CEMETERY

Manila

Consecrated 1945

"MILE LONG" BARRACKS AND AMERICAN HOSPITAL
Corregidor Island
Bombed 1942

BATTERY HEARN/12-INCH AMERICAN GUN
Corregidor Island
Captured 1942

BATTERY GRUBBS/AMERICAN "DISAPPEARING" GUN
Corregidor Island
Disabled 1942

FORT DRUM/AMERICAN "ISLAND BATTLESHIP"
Manila Bay
Captured 1942

NORTH EXIT/MACARTHUR'S HEADQUARTERS
Malinta Tunnel/Corregidor Island
Surrendered 1942

LATERAL N-1/MACARTHUR'S HEADQUARTERS
Malinta Tunnel/Corregidor Island
Surrendered 1942

FORT BONIFACIO/AMERICAN MILITARY CEMETERY
Manila
Consecrated 1945

I N A SWEET VOICE, redolent of her native Kentucky and a lifetime as a nurse, Sallie Farmer can recount matter-of-factly the fall of Manila, the months in the Malinta Tunnel and three years as prisoner in the Philippines. Mrs. Farmer, then Sallie Phillips Durrett, joined the Army Nurse Corps in 1937. In June 1941, the Army sent her to the Philippines as a surgical nurse in the station hospital. "We were aware there was trouble brewing with Japan, but we thought it would be over in two or three months. We arrived in Manila on Christmas Day, 1941. That day, MacArthur declared Manila an Open City. We boarded a boat and set sail the next morning. I worked in Bataan for three months. The day before the surrender, we were ordered to go to Corregidor."

She worked in the "hospital"—one of the laterals—of the Malinta Tunnel until Corregidor surrendered on 6 May '42. The Japanese came in, in asbestos suits, with flamethrowers at the ready, in case there was any resistance. But there was none. In Manila, the Japanese separated the nurses and they took us in trucks to San Tomás. It had been a university owned by the Spanish Dominican Fathers. During the time I was there, I didn't see any physical abuse. It was more a situation of neglect. We were low on food and they didn't bring any extra. The same was true of medical supplies."

Throughout her imprisonment Sallie kept one small measure of control over her destiny. Prior to the war, she became engaged to a fellow officer in the Philippines, Gerry C. Burett of the Field Artillery. She secreted the ring in an empty gas mask case she kept with her during the years at San Tomás. "That ring meant a lot to me and I just didn't think they had a right to take it away." Burett died aboard a Japanese prison ship in December 1944. She was interviewed, after the war, by a local Ohio Catholic newspaper. The reporter was named Joseph Farmer.

SALLIE PHILLIPS DURRETT FARMER
NURSE
U.S. Army Nurse Corps
1937–1946

When Clark Field was bombed, three miles from her hospital, "there were about ten wounded. We worked from 1 P.M. to 1 A.M. in surgery. There were no shelters, so we just lay down under the porch of the operating room," at Ft. Stotsenburg, "and slept." She was evacuated to Bataan, then to Corregidor and—with the surrender of the American forces—to imprisonment at San Tomás University in Manila until American forces returned.

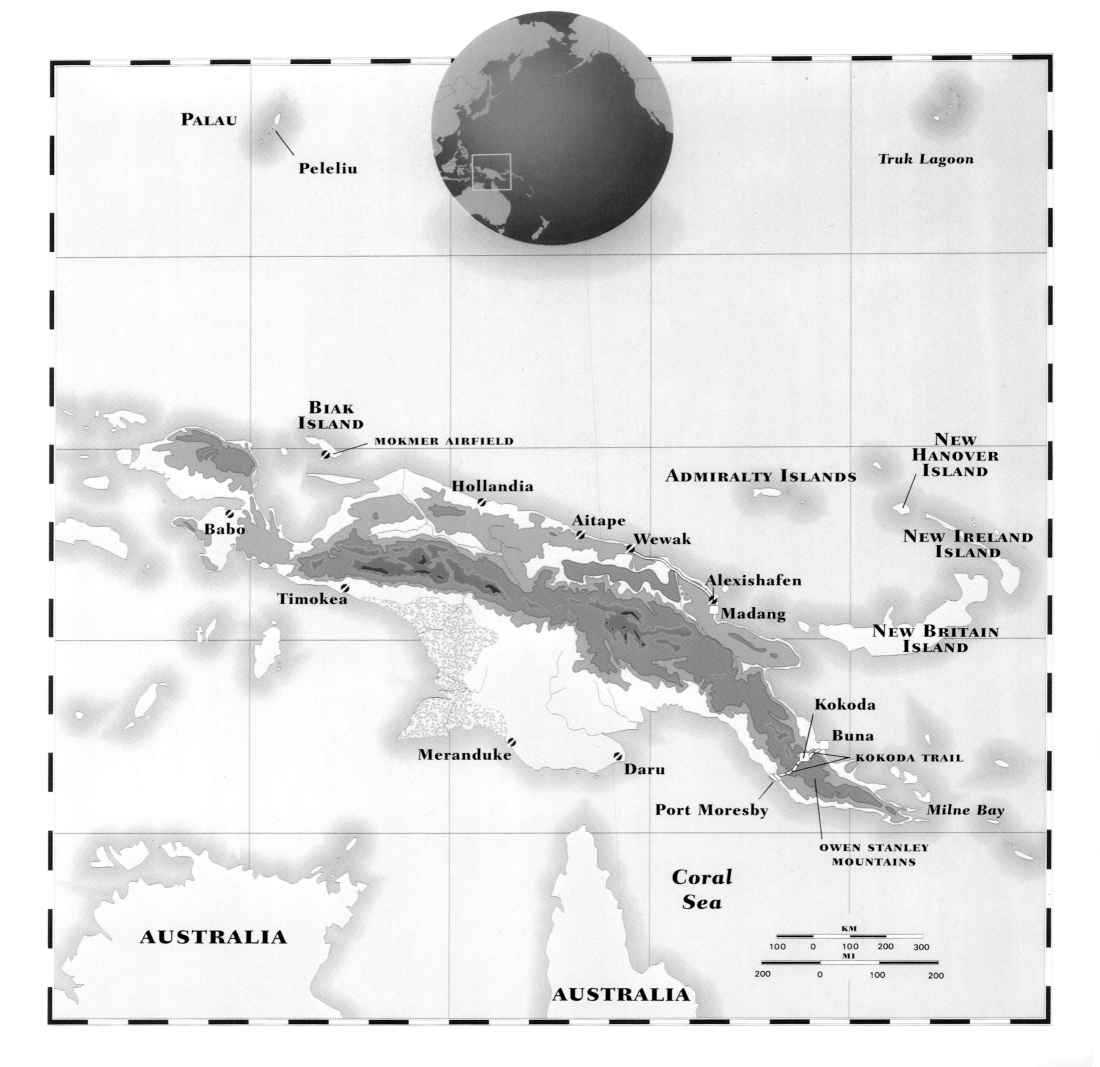

PALAU

Peleliu

Truk Lagoon

BIAK
ISLAND

MOKMER AIRFIELD

NEW
HANOVER
ISLAND

Hollandia

ADMIRALTY ISLANDS

Babo

Aitape

Wewak

NEW IRELAND
ISLAND

Alexishafen

Timokea

Madang

NEW BRITAIN
ISLAND

Kokoda

Buna

Meranduke

KOKODA TRAIL

Daru

Milne Bay

Port Moresby

OWEN STANLEY
MOUNTAINS

Coral
Sea

AUSTRALIA

KM

100   0   100   200   300
MI

200   0   100   200

AUSTRALIA

THE KEYSTONE: New Guinea dominates the Solomons—and the western sea lanes to Australia. THE FEAT: Australian engineers built the "Golden Staircase" across the Owen Stanley Mountains—a 4,000-step highway. THE AUSTRALIANS: The "Diggers" raced from the desert heat of the fight against Rommel's Afrika Corps to the fetid jungles and the defense of their home, the protracted fingernail-by-fingernail gouging that was warfare on the Kokoda Trail. THE AMERICANS: Green, as was their commander, MacArthur, but ready to show their stuff and fully aware that troops they tied down here would not be reinforcements at "the 'Canal." THE JAPANESE: Half-starved at the end, bereft of weapons, ammunition, medicine; covering themselves in rice sacks; 13,000 perished. THE COST: 2,100 Diggers died, 3,500 were wounded. Of the Americans, 950 were killed or lost in action. Another 2,000 were wounded.

THE WORLD'S SECOND-LARGEST ISLAND, twice the size of California, half-again larger than France, New Guinea lies over the north of Australia like a dozing salamander. To control New Guinea is to control the Island Continent. MacArthur knew it. Japanese military planners knew it; in February 1942 they bombed the Australian port of Darwin.

Forces of the Chrysanthemum Throne quickly occupied the northern half of this inestimably rugged island. They established their headquarters at Buna. Allied forces, on the south coast, made their nerve center at Port Moresby.

Between them were the Owen Stanley Mountains and a slender track under jungle canopy, a festering battle corridor with a name that bespeaks its jungle wilderness: the Kokoda Trail.

"Kokoda?" in Japanese is "Where are you?" A call in the impenetrable forest. "Koko*da!*" or "I'm *here!*" was the expected answer.

It was along this trail, at places with names like Wairopi (pidgin for "wire rope"—the bridge at hand) and Rouna Falls, that Australian "Diggers" and their American comrades fought to protect Australia. Both sides suf-fered in humid heat that rotted clothes on the soldiers' backs. Both sides watched comrades suffer piteously for the lack of medicines to stem infection, disease, and pain of wounds. If malaria is one of the torments of Hell, the strain was cultured on New Guinea.

Fighting for control of New Guinea meant ejecting the Japanese from a coastline fortified along its 1,200-mile length. To supply troops as they moved northward, Allied engineers accomplished one of the engineering marvels of the war. They cut a 4,000-step staircase into the steep slopes of the Owen Stanley range.

Japanese forces, however, would not oblige by remaining static in defensive positions. In an effort to drive the Allies back to Australia, plans were laid to land Japanese troops at Port Moresby. The best-laid plans, however, are sometimes read by the other side.

Japanese naval codes were broken just prior to Pearl Harbor and—even prior to Midway—intelligence analysts scored their first coup by learning of the Port Moresby operation. The landing forces were intercepted in the Battle of the Coral Sea (May 4–8, 1942) and turned back.

From Cape Gloucester to the Owen Stanley Mountains to the Coral Sea, the battle for New Guinea was the battle for Australia, but also an epic struggle of wills for survival.

◖ ◖ ◖

The Battle of the Coral Sea was the first encounter in naval history where the opposing ships were never in sight of each other. The aircraft carrier was now the dominant factor in naval warfare.

B-17 FLYING FORTRESS
Black Cat Pass
Disappeared 1942

IMITA RIDGE
Kokoda Trail/Owen Stanley Mountains
Assaulted 1942

EMPENNAGE/JAPANESE FIGHTER PLANE
Near Danip
Crashed 1943

The Japanese ground troops left in the north pushed south regardless, and September found them only thirty miles from Port Moresby. The Allied forces mounted an offensive, and were gaining ground by the end of the year. After capturing airfields in the north, they were able to reinforce quickly and started to make significant gains. Buna finally fell in January of 1943.

Discussion of the battle in recent times has centered, however, not on the outcome of the fight, but on a particular aspect of its aftermath.

First, American forces found—for the first time—that they were the equal of their foe. More important, modern analysts have focused on the damage sustained by the carrier *Yorktown*. The battle ended on May 8, 1942, and her captain estimated the *Yorktown* would need ninety days to return to the line.

Working feverishly, workmen accomplished satisfactory repairs and returned the carrier to duty in forty-

five *hours*. The *Yorktown* went on to play a pivotal, if sacrificial, role in the "Miracle at Midway" on June 4. With American industry faced with economic competition from superior Japanese products and strategists in recent years, more than one analyst and commentator have recalled the *Yorktown*'s forty-five-hour repairs. They have wondered out loud what happened to the ingenuity and "can do" attitude those workmen displayed in that critical 1942 juncture.

Following the Battle of the Coral Sea, the struggle for New Guinea flowed westward. It moved closer to the head of the salamander—some call it a bird—that MacArthur coveted as his jumping-off point for a return to the Philippines.

It was to be a long struggle. It was April of 1944 before Hollandia was secured, and almost August until the fiercely defended airfield at Biak was taken.

◊ ◊ ◊

The battle for New Guinea did not draw to its close until August 1944, after fighting that lasted more than half of the war. Even then, the Japanese commander, Lt. Gen. Hatazo Adachi, retreated to the jungle and waged guerrilla war until a radio dispatch informed him of his country's surrender.

◊ ◊ ◊

MITSUBISHI G4M ("BETTY") BOMBER
Near Danip
Crashed 1943

NORTH OF THE GOLDIE RIVER
Owen Stanley Mountains
Traversed 1942

B-17 FLYING FORTRESS
Black Cat Pass
Disappeared 1942

JAPANESE LIGHT BOMBER
Alexishafen
Disabled 1943

MUCH PRAISE HAS BEEN DESERVEDLY bestowed upon the Americans of Japanese ancestry who fought with such distinction in Europe. The "Go for Broke" 442nd Regimental Combat Team was one of the most decorated Army units in Europe—even as the 127,000 Americans of Japanese descent were being herded into camps for the war's duration. Lesser known, in part by design, was the clandestine contribution of "Issei" (Japan-born Americans), "Nisei" (Amer-icans born of Japanese parents), and "Kibei" (American-born, but educated in Japan). On MacArthur's staff, they were called "America's secret weapon" in the Pacific. Steve Yamamoto was one of those secret weapons. "I knew my number was coming up soon, so I volunteered and entered the service in March 1941. Subsequently I embarked on an intelligence career," which included twenty years of service in uniform.

Yamamoto's Army career included service as a translator at the Tokyo war crimes trials. He retired as a lieutenant colonel and later joined the Defense Intelligence Agency, where he remained for another twenty-five years. Yamamoto supervised or personally conducted the interrogation of an astounding 3,100 prisoners on New Guinea, yielding information that proved indispensable to the success of air operations in the campaign. His efforts earned him the Bronze Star.

"I felt privileged to be doing that kind of work. The prisoners, however, would look at me oddly. They felt that only in the American Army could a Japanese be given a position of that responsibility. Many of them said they would talk, but asked me to take my pistol afterward and shoot them. They said they could not go home to Japan after having been taken prisoner. I answered that they would be able to go home; that they should not be ashamed. Because by the time they returned, Japan would be a defeated nation. In general, they were very cooperative. They were well treated and felt honor-bound to answer our questions."

LIEUTENANT COLONEL STEVE YAMAMOTO

INTERROGATOR
U.S. Army
1941–1961

I was one of sixty-one Nisei for a first-of-its-kind intelligence school. That was in November of 1941. On December 7, what was originally a one-year course became six months." Captured prisoners were well treated and often cooperative. They were fed on captured Japanese rations, which cooks often saved for Yamamoto, too. After catching a prisoner in a deception, "I felt confident."

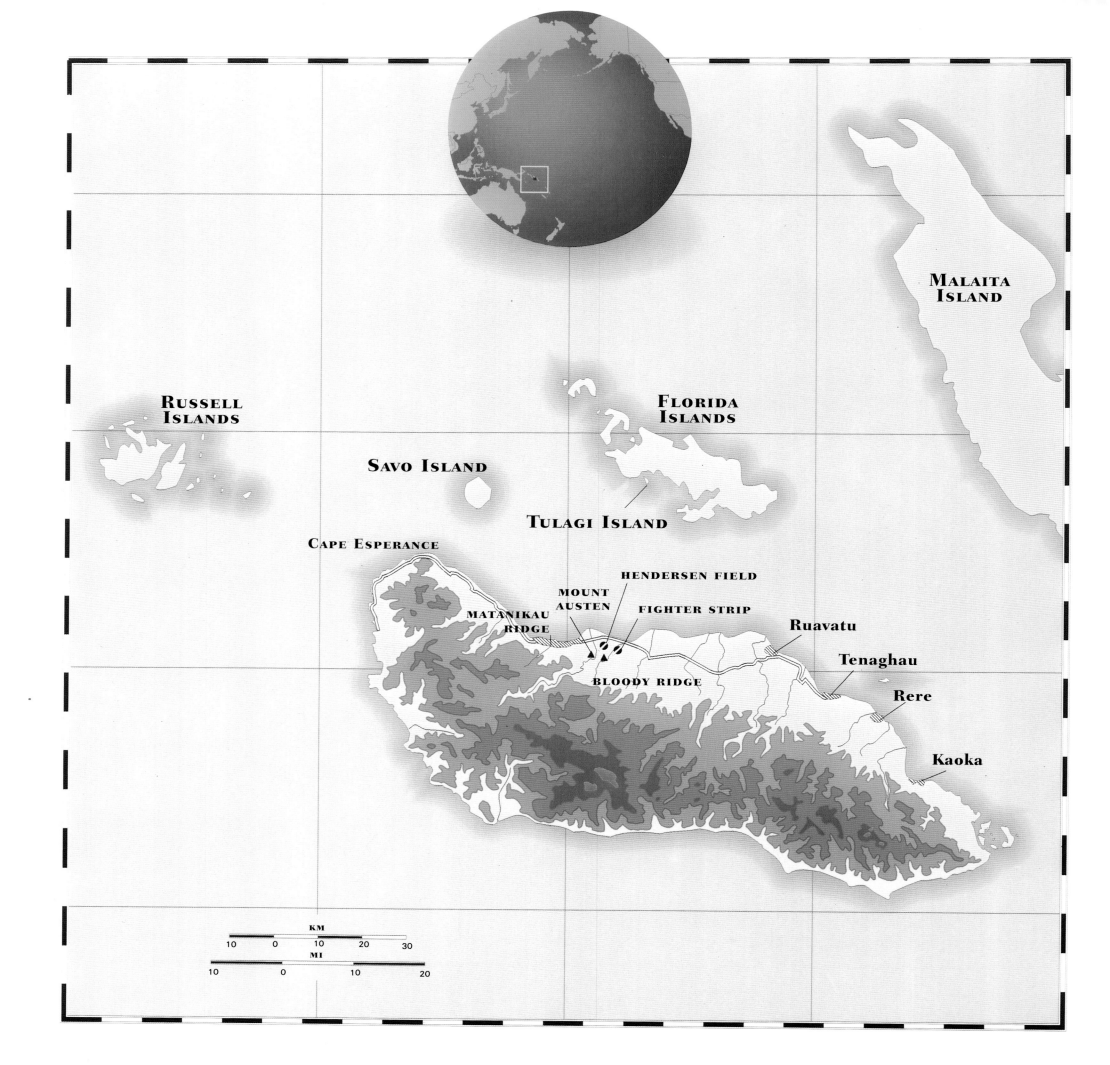

MALAITA
ISLAND

RUSSELL
ISLANDS

FLORIDA
ISLANDS

SAVO ISLAND

TULAGI ISLAND

CAPE ESPERANCE

HENDERSEN FIELD

MOUNT
AUSTEN

MATANIKAU
RIDGE

FIGHTER STRIP

Ruavatu

Tenaghau

BLOODY RIDGE

Rere

Kaoka

KM

10   0   10   20   30

MI

10   0   10   20

ガダルカナル

THE TEST: Would America seek an early peace or fight to total victory? THE DOUBTS: Fighting raged nearly six months, from August 1942. THE DEFEAT: Savo Island, nearly 2,000 American casualties in one night. THE PRIZE: Henderson Field, the airstrip that was crucial to the American victory; needed for resupply, the raison d'être of the battle. TOTAL WAR: It was a fight for control of air, land, and sea, with bravery and confusion evident in equal measure. FIRST VICTORY: Americans repulsed a Japanese attack at the Ilu River, the first time they defeated a Japanese force.

SARATOGA, ANTIETAM, AND TET, to name a few. In many, if not all, of America's wars, there was a watershed battle. A battle after which there would either be a sapping of the will to continue, as there was after Tet—or a renewed resolve to carry the fight forward.

Guadalcanal was a defining moment of World War II. It was a see-saw battle, with victory against a ferocious and efficient foe far from assured. And it was fought against the backdrop of the difficult midterm 1942 congressional elections. With American forces yet to commit to North African or European battles en masse, headlines painted daily stories of the struggle in the Solomons. It was less than a year after Pearl Harbor, but echoes of isolationist sentiment still infused public debate, and the will to unconditional victory had yet to congeal.

For the Americans, Guadalcanal would be the first attempt to wrest territory back from the Japanese. For the Chrysanthemum Throne, its vital airstrip (called Henderson Field by the Americans) made the island the gateway to the Coral Sea and the prize of Australia beyond it. On August 7, 1942, the marines landed. The battle was joined.

Celebrated in Richard Tregaskis's 1943 book *Guadalcanal Diary* and a subsequent movie, the 'Canal was more than a test of men and machines. It was a crucible of American political will.

◊ ◊ ◊

For a good part of the seven-month battle, it was the focal point of the Pacific conflict. A contest on land, sea, and air, it was perhaps the most intense naval campaign that the world had ever seen.

At sea, well-trained, audacious Japanese mariners fought to clear the way for the resupply of their garrison defending the island. For a period, they succeeded and Americans dubbed the stream of reinforcements and matériel the "Tokyo Express."

Opening the way for the delivery train, however, was the climactic Battle of Savo Island. The cone-shaped hummock lies across a body of water from the 'Canal. The body of water is now called Ironbottom Sound, because in less than an hour in the early morning of August 9 Japanese naval gunners killed 1,270 American sailors and wounded 700 more.

Japanese commanders on land, however, often squandered the tenacity of their men. Instead of mounting a concentrated attack, they committed forces piecemeal—judgment that earned them history's denigration.

One climactic assault became famous in American households. Seeking to deny the vital Henderson Field airstrip to the Americans, a Japanese force of 1,000 men tried three times, over fourteen hours, to breach the marines' perimeter. Not 200 survived; their commander committed ritual suicide.

ILU SANDSPIT
Mouth of Ilu River
Assaulted 1942

Americans fastened on the battle because it was the first time their fighting men had defeated Japanese forces. But it was far from decisive in the struggle for control of Guadalcanal. The attrition of malaria, dengue fever, dysentery, and exhaustion thinned the ranks of both sides. Each side struggled—and succeeded—in landing reinforcements and clearing the seas and skies of the enemy.

In late October the situation remained so precarious—and the American commitment to concentrate on Hitler's defeat as first priority so inviolate—that Roosevelt himself had to intervene with his generals and ensure the beleaguered Guadalcanal garrison would get the men and arms it needed.

The decision came at a crucial point in the fray, the battle for Bloody Ridge, the high ground overlooking Henderson Field. Troops under Marine Lt. Col. Eugene "Chesty" Puller were forced into a perimeter of only several hundred yards. The Japanese attacked, as usual, with tremendous bravery but poor planning. By the time they gave up, they had left 2,000 dead and perhaps 5,000 wounded. American losses were under 300. The marines went on the offensive, and the fighting continued at a savage pace. Hours after Puller regrouped on Bloody Ridge, the naval Battle of the Santa Cruz Islands was under way. It would cost the United States the carrier *Hornet*, launch pad of the Doolittle Raid.

Japanese forces made one more major effort to land reinforcements, in November. The three-day naval Battle of Guadalcanal cost America thirteen ships, including two battleships and one heavy cruiser.

But it also gained the country something. Though it would be February before Japanese forces evacuated their positions on Guadalcanal, the climactic fight offshore sealed the fate of the Pacific War.

The cruiser sunk was the *Juneau*, torpedoed on Saturday, November 14, 1942, and it was unique in the annals of the U.S. Navy. Among the shipmates lost with the *Juneau* were the five Sullivan brothers.

◊ ◊ ◊

The calm resolve of the parents of the "Fighting Sullivans" sobered the nation when the loss of their five sons on the *Juneau* was announced in January 1943. It also steeled America for the fighting ahead. The turning point had been reached.

◊ ◊ ◊

AMERICAN BARBED WIRE
Bloody Ridge
Emplaced 1942

JAPANESE COASTAL GUN
Red Beach
Assaulted 1942

AMERICAN AIR TRAFFIC
CONTROL TOWER
Henderson Field
Erected 1942

AMERICAN LANDING CRAFT
Abandoned 1942

MARSDEN MATTING
Construction material for American airstrips
Recycled 1990

BLOODY RIDGE
Defended 1942

FATHER ELMER HEINDL is one of the most decorated chaplains of World War II, or any war for that matter; he reluctantly enumerates his decorations: two Distinguished Service Crosses, the Silver Star, the Bronze Star, and the Legion of Merit. In more than two years of Army duty in combat zones, including Guadalcanal, New Britain, Bougainville, and the Philippines, he only saw his duty as to serve. A noncombatant, he won his decorations for the risks he took to reach the wounded or unaccounted for and bring them spiritual comfort. He was already ordained and a youth leader in his Rochester parish when war broke out.

"I saw many of my young people were being drafted. . . . I was gratified to take care of them, to tend to their spiri-

tual needs in a church manner . . . to help them as they went off to war."

Repeatedly under fire, he found "extreme trust in Providence, and secondly, trust in the competence, training, dedication, and devotion of my comrades. There are no bonds stronger, more abiding, or more sincerely placed than those of people in combat. You're facing the great unknown, in which anything can happen at any moment."

Those bonds, of course, were forged in a "parish" of many faiths, many feelings, beliefs, convictions. For Heindl, "it was a wonderful experience to see how full of faith these people were. In my mind, for us chaplains, there's only one God. We pray to that one God, no matter how we express that faith. Our job is to help that person find his own God."

FATHER ELMER HEINDL
CHAPLAIN
U.S. Army Chaplain Corps
1942–1949

There are no atheists in foxholes. None believe that more than chaplains—volunteers, not sitting in judgment of souls but balming them or easing their exit from the torn world. And not probing—or even identifying—the faith of soldiers. We were there to serve, says the Rev. Elmer Heindl, a highly decorated chaplain and veteran of Guadalcanal, the Solomons, and the Philippines.

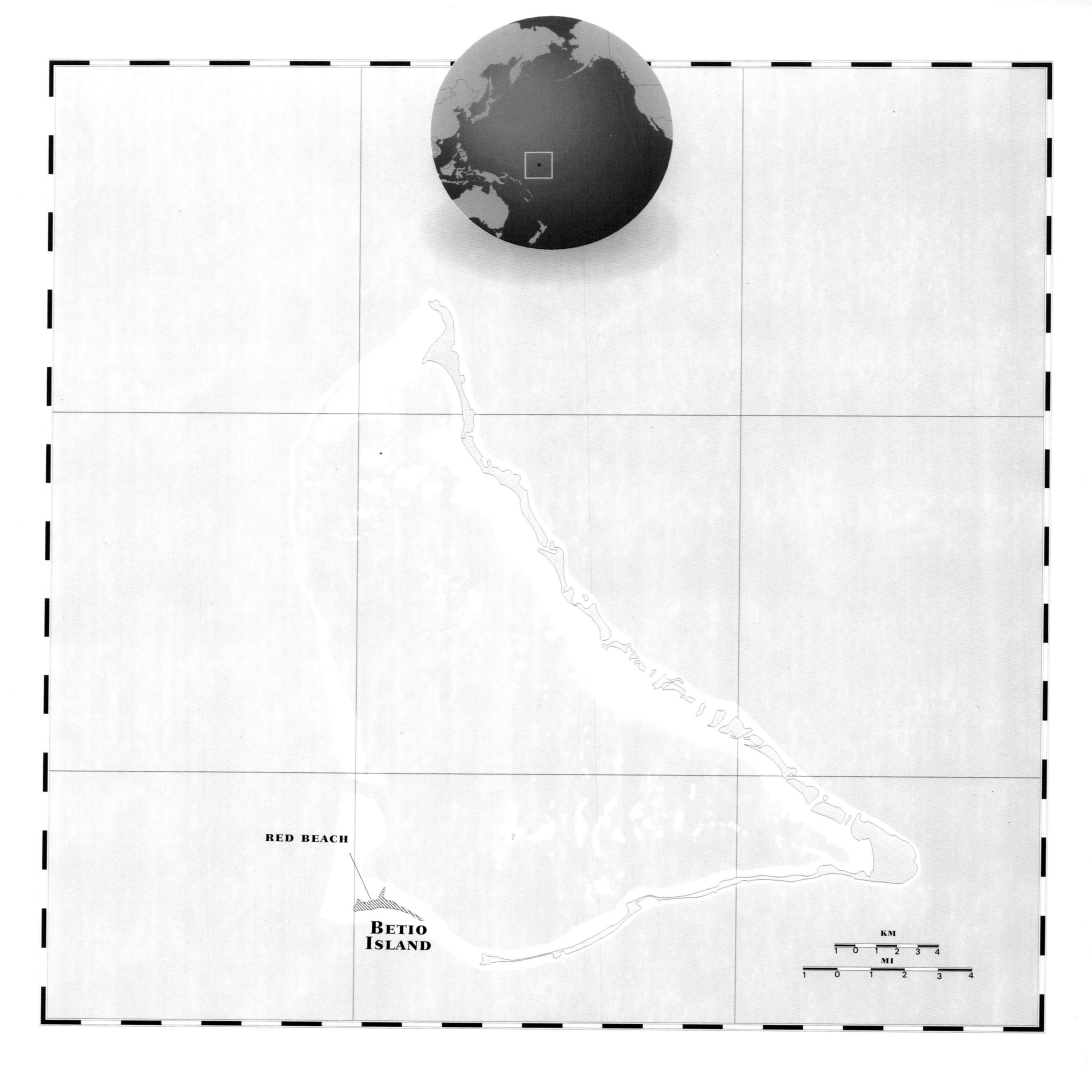

RED BEACH

**BETIO
ISLAND**

KM
1 0 1 2 3 4
MI
1 0 1 2 3 4

THE SOBRIQUET: Call it "Bloody Tarawa." THE OBSTACLE: Poor intelligence did not account for tides or offshore reefs. Heavily laden marines were forced to swim 700 yards to the beach, under withering enemy fire. THE OUTCRY: Casualty ratios of 1:1 caused doubt of marine tactics and prompted congressional scrutiny. THE PHOTOS: Americans saw pictures of their war dead for the first time. THE DEAD: Nearly all 4,700 Japanese; 900 Americans. About 146 Japanese were taken prisoner; 2,100 Americans were wounded in the week-long battle.

JAPANESE COASTAL GUNS
Southern beach/Betio Island
Sold to Japan by Great Britain 1903

AMONG THE MANY popular nominees as "oxymorons"—words or phrases that appear to be inherently contradictory—is "military intelligence." Never was this joke so grim as in "Bloody Tarawa."

Vital for their airstrips in the mid-Pacific, the Gilbert Islands—today an independent nation called Kiribati (pidgin for Gilbert)—were "controlled" militarily by the Tarawa Atoll. And the key to them was the tiny island of Betio.

Photo reconnaissance prefacing the invasion was superb. At first, military intelligence did its job: Aerial and submarine pictures of the defenses spotted a latrine. Resolving the image and counting "heads"—one could say—yielded the number of defenders on the island.

Natives of the atoll were enthusiastic supporters of the American "invaders." They paddled out to the invasion force and gave clear instructions on tides and routes through, or over, the coral reefs forming a yoke around Betio, about 500 yards offshore.

This was November 1943. Amphibious warfare was still relatively new. American "intelligence" didn't know whether or not to trust the natives. The would-be scouts were ignored and the landing craft were sent in at low tide and grounded on reefs hundreds of yards from shore. The

marines had to wade in full field packs—often in chest-high water—directly into enemy fire. It was a charnel house.

The battle lasted a week. In this brief purgatory, the marines lost 900 dead and about 2,400 wounded. Of 5,000 men assaulting Betio the first day, one in ten was killed outright; another 1,000 were wounded. (Eight months later, 152,000 troops would land on the five famous beaches at Normandy; there were 12,000 wounded the first day and 2,500 killed.)

The Japanese garrison was virtually annihilated—a trend repeated throughout the Pacific campaign. On Tarawa, 4,700 Japanese died. Only 146 were taken alive. The casualty ratio, what would in a later war be called a "body count," came to nearly 1:1. A hue and cry erupted at home. The marines became more sensitive to their image as reckless expenders of American life. But the casualties would mount.

It was after Tarawa, too, that American censors allowed pictures of American dead on the battlefield. Pictures of "our boys" in the surf at the island edge provoked an understandable round of criticism on the home front. Troops in combat wondered what the fuss was about. The bodies in the photographs were intact.

Perhaps no other theater of the war knew a greater, more intense, more avoidable disaster. Cruel arithmetic says the battle for Betio left about twenty men dead for every acre of ground.

◊ ◊ ◊

The now-infamous reefs of Tarawa were far from a one-time obstacle. Landing craft had to make the trip from ship to shore repeatedly, hauling ammunition, wounded, fresh troops and even the British governor who restored his country's sovereignty.

JAPANESE TANK
Red Beach
Destroyed 1943

AMERICAN DEBRIS
Red Beach
Abandoned 1943

JAPANESE FIRING POSITION
Southern beach/Betio Island
Constructed 1943

AMERICAN LANDING CRAFT
Red Beach
Sunk 1943

"TARAWA WAS SUPPOSED to be a duck soup operation. . . . No one knew what these island-hoppings would be," Frey recalls. A Navy motorman, he was on a landing craft in the first wave of the disastrous assault.

"It was calm," but there were delays before 9 or 10 A.M., when the landing craft started in toward the beaches. Tarawa had a long pier and "we thought you could just drop 'em off" and head back.

Instead, in an intelligence and planning failure which still haunts marine doctrine, the landing craft became fouled on reefs about 700 to 1,000 yards off the beaches. "We thought we were on shore," but "hell, your props were gone and you were out." The craft were stranded under fire. Frey remembers thinking, "They're

going to kill us! They're shooting at us!" before being towed out of range.

Though Tarawa was largely a marine operation, chance had it that Frey would later land amphibious troops of the Army's Seventh Infantry Division, which brought him a small role in one of the historic moments

of World War II. Today a salesman of water-pumping systems and windmills, Frey's voice takes on a youthful timbre as he recounts that he was in the lead landing craft at Leyte Gulf. He was given the assignment to radio the message "Brunswick One has landed." American forces had returned to the Philippines. About three hours later, MacArthur waded ashore. Thinking back on the troops he ferried to the beaches at Tarawa and later, Frey observes, "I'd hate to say they were heroes. They were just survivors."

WALTER FREY
LST MOTOR MACHINIST'S MATE
U.S. Navy
1943–1945

The landing craft on which he was a motorman was disabled not once, but twice, on the bloody reefs at Tarawa. The first time was a snagged propeller, but the second happened when a tank crew began to disembark before the ramp was lowered. "These guys were scared crapless. They were buttoned up inside a Sherman tank. If we went down, they were gone."

ADMIRALTY ISLANDS

NEW HANOVER

NEW IRELAND

Bismarck Sea

Rabaul

CAPE LAMBERT

Simpson Harbor

LONG ISLAND

UMBOI ISLAND

CAPE GLOUCESTER

Talasea

Hoskins

Wide Bay

Jaquinot Bay

Vitiaz Str.

Dampier Str.

Arawe

Gasmata

NEW GUINEA

KM
25 0 25 50 75

MI
25 0 25 50

ラバウル/ニューブリテン

THE OPERATION: "Cartwheel." THE GOAL: To isolate the 100,000-man garrison at Rabaul. THE LEGEND: Navy Lt. (jg) Edward "Butch" O'Hare, aviator, ace, Medal of Honor winner. THE STRATEGY: A daring leap from Hawaii to the Gilbert Islands' airfield at Tarawa. THE TACTICS: Envelop the installation, headquarters of a Japanese Army group and a major air and naval center. From 1942 to the middle of 1944, "Operation Cartwheel" drew a deadly seine, from New Guinea to Guadalcanal and from New Britain to Bougainville.

CLAUSEWITZ, THE PRUSSIAN SOLDIER-SCHOLAR, admonishes that in war the objective is to destroy the enemy's army. Generations of generals trained under his tutelage, but the "book" was discarded at Rabaul.

Headquarters of a Japanese Army group and a major air and naval center, Rabaul would have been a prize conquest to any disciple of Clausewitz. Allied commanders, however, decided to envelop Rabaul and, much as the boa constrictor suffocates its prey, leave 100,000 men to languish under air and sea attack. General Tojo himself saw the strategy firsthand, when he came under air attack while touring Rabaul in the summer of 1942.

The plan of the Allies was to deny the Japanese sanctuary at Rabaul. Gradually, from 1942 to the middle of 1944, a purse was tightened, from New Guinea's rugged terrain to the Ilu Sandspit on Guadalcanal and from Cape Gloucester—at the opposite end of New Britain—to Bougainville.

◖ ◖ ◖

Here, Allied airpower proved its integral role in the island-hopping strategy. General Tojo himself came under bombardment, in the summer of '42, on an inspection tour.

◖ ◖ ◖

Each of these objectives in the operation, code-named Cartwheel and launched in June 1943, had a separate rationale. Guadalcanal, of course, controlled the Solomons and the westward approach to Australia. Bougainville was the Japanese administrative headquarters in the Solomon Islands. It was also a key military center in its own right. In April 1943, U.S. code crackers deciphered the itinerary of a forthcoming tour by Adm. Isoroku Yamamoto—the reluctant warrior who was the architect of the Pearl Harbor attack and the defeat at Midway. After some debate, a flight of fighter planes was dispatched to intercept Yamamoto.

The story is quite famous—and sometimes controversial. Authoritative accounts have it that a flight of sixteen P-38 "Lightnings" from Guadalcanal's Henderson Field found Yamamoto right on schedule. Lt. Thomas Lanphier picked one of the two "Betty" bombers escorted by six Japanese fighters and shot its right wing off. The plane crashed on Bougainville, where

JAPANESE LIGHT BOMBER
Lakunai Airfield/Rabaul
Disabled 1944

Yamamoto's remains were recovered by a Japanese search. The wreckage of the plane is marked and well known, though civil insurrection has made it difficult to reach.

Cape Gloucester needed to be secured to control the Dampier Strait and the nearby Vitaz Strait—the twin southern gateways to the Bismarck Sea. In bitter homage to the German chancellor, the promontory was taken and defended with "iron and blood."

A legend was also born—and died—in the battle over and around Rabaul. On February 25, 1942, a task force from the carrier *Lexington* bat-tled Rabaul-based bombers. His wingman's guns jammed, Navy Lt. (jg) Edward "Butch" O'Hare fought alone against nine Japanese planes.

O'Hare downed five of them, in one action becoming America's first air ace and winning the Medal of Honor.

◊ ◊ ◊

MacArthur thirsted for additional troops to root the Japanese from their base at Rabaul. When the Allied leadership met at the Casablanca conference at the beginning of 1943, however, his goals were blocked. American troop strength in Europe numbered about 380,000, while there were nearly a half million in the Pacific Theater. MacArthur improvised and launched Operation Cartwheel in June.

◊ ◊ ◊

The isolation of Rabaul made possible the daring leap across the Pacific from Hawaii to the Gilbert Islands and Tarawa in November 1943.

It was over Makin Island, in the Gilberts campaign, that O'Hare was shot down and killed. His home city, Chicago, named its airport for him.

UNEXPLODED AMERICAN ORDNANCE

Rabaul

Impacted 1944

JAPANESE ANTIAIRCRAFT GUN
Above Simpson Harbor/Rabaul
Abandoned 1944

JAPANESE AIRPLANE WING
Lakunai Airfield/Rabaul
Severed 1944

JAPANESE COASTAL GUN
Above Simpson Harbor/Rabaul
Abandoned 1944

AIRPOWER WAS KEY TO the entire strategy of the Pacific War. Sea battle after sea battle was waged not by gunners but by pilots from opposing aircraft carriers.

The Marianas were assaulted as a potential base for strategic bombing missions; Iwo Jima was seized as a way station and fighter base. The island-hopping theory—even when Billy Mitchell first articulated it—called for leaps from airstrip to airstrip.

From the earliest days of the war, the Third Air Wing of the Marine Corps, initially based in Midway, ranged the Pacific, playing its vital role. Regis was a mechanic in the Third Air Wing, having sneaked into the marines while under age.

"I was sixteen when I joined," and became an aviation mechanic. "But I turned seventeen when I was in boot camp, so by the time they found out about it, it didn't matter anymore."

Regis served three and a half years and went on to a career as a professional dancer, owner of a chain of Arthur Murray dance studios, and maître d' in a casino in Las Vegas.

MARIO REGIS
AVIATION MECHANIC
U.S. Marine Corps
1941–1945

"I was sixteen when I joined," and became an aviation mechanic. "But I turned seventeen when I was in boot camp, so by the time they found out about it, it didn't matter anymore." A city kid who joined up in search of adventure, Regis got it by the eyeful. He was already on Midway when the epic battle was fought.

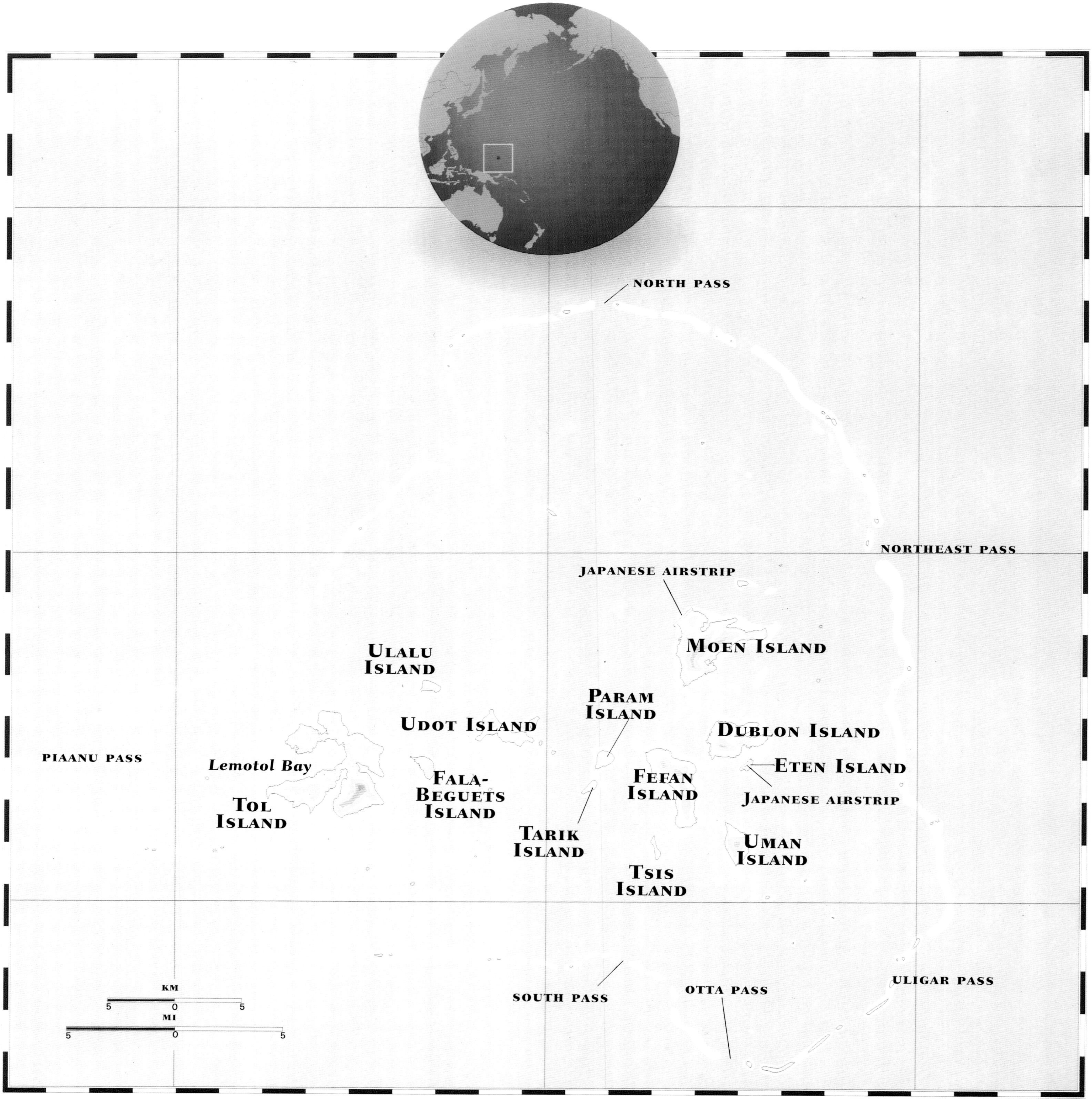

NORTH PASS

NORTHEAST PASS

JAPANESE AIRSTRIP

MOEN ISLAND

ULALU ISLAND

PARAM ISLAND

UDOT ISLAND

DUBLON ISLAND

PIAANU PASS

Lemotol Bay

ETEN ISLAND

FALA-BEGUETS ISLAND

FEFAN ISLAND

JAPANESE AIRSTRIP

TOL ISLAND

TARIK ISLAND

UMAN ISLAND

TSIS ISLAND

KM

5   0   5

MI

5   0   5

SOUTH PASS   OTTA PASS   ULIGAR PASS

THE LAGOON: Japan's combined fleet headquarters.
THE BOMBARDMENT: By air and battlewagon guns, on
February 17 and 18, 1944. THE LOSSES: About 250 Japanese
aircraft, 15 warships, and 137,000 tons of merchant shipping.
THE RETREAT: Naval administrative and support units were
removed to Rabaul, where they languished for the duration of the
war. THE WRECKAGE: Today, Truk Lagoon is a popular destination
for divers, who pore over the wrecks of planes, trucks, and ships
left to little but rust, tides, and countless forms of sea life.

MOEN, ETEN, AND DUBLON ISLANDS
Truk Lagoon
Bombed and Shelled 1944

IN SONG AND CRY, the refrain of "Remember Pearl Harbor" was heard throughout America's war in the Pacific. If anywhere, Pearl Harbor was avenged at Truk Lagoon.

Site of Japan's Combined Fleet headquarters, Truk had been the object of American raids by carrier-based planes and scores of submarine surveillance and attack missions.

In fact, it was the sinking of a Japanese cruiser by an American submarine in early February 1944 that gave the Imperial Navy an inkling of the massive attack to come. The Combined Fleet fled west, but left much behind.

Soldiers and marines had just secured the Kwajalein Atoll and GI's were wading ashore at Eniwetok, 700 miles away, when air and naval forces zeroed in on Truk on February 17 and 18, 1944.

◊ ◊ ◊

When American soldiers seized control of the Marshall Islands, conquering Kwajalein and Eniwetok atolls in February of 1944, the Truk base became untenable and had to be abandoned. To a Japanese commentator, it was as if the British had been forced to evacuate Gibraltar.

◊ ◊ ◊

The battlewagons *Iowa* and *New Jersey* circled the outer rim of the atoll. Their 16-inch guns hurled one-ton shells more than twenty miles—so far that gunners had to account for the rotation of the Earth while the projectile was in flight.

Four carriers launched their planes on February 18. When the carnage ended, about 350 Japanese aircraft, 15 warships, and 137,000 tons of merchant shipping were sunk. Truk would never again be a fleet headquarters.

The brunt of the defeat had to be borne by Adm. Mineichi Koga. He had assumed fleet command on the death of Yamamoto. Like his predecessor, he was only reluctant at the advent of war.

In particular, he protested that those who would do the most fighting—and dying—had been the least consulted by the militants who had precipitated the conflict.

TRUCK/SANKISAN MARU
West of Uman Island
Sunk 1944

MITSUBISHI ZERO ("ZEKE") FIGHTER PLANE
Northeast coast/Eten Island
Crashed 1944

MITSUBISHI G4M ("BETTY") BOMBER
Southwest of Eten Island
Crashed 1944

PROPELLER/GOSEI MARU
Northeast of Uman Island
Sunk 1944

DECK GUN/HINO MARU #2

West of Uman Island

Sunk 1944

COCKPIT/YOKOSUKA D4Y ("JUDY") DIVE BOMBER
Northeast coast/Eten Island
Crashed 1944

EMPENNAGE/YOKOSUKA D4Y ("JUDY") DIVE BOMBER
North of Eten Island
Crashed 1944

JAPANESE NAVAL HOSPITAL
Eten Island
Surrendered 1945

A VITAL JAPANESE NAVAL BASE in the central Pacific, the Truk Lagoon was bypassed by American land forces, then harassed by constant air and submarine attacks. Kess served in the engine room of one of those submarines, the USS *Drum*. He was part of a small, lethal, and elite fighting force. It was known as the "Silent Service."

The foundation of the American submarine service was laid down as early as the 1920s. Examining the records of the lethal and dreaded German U-boats of World War I, American naval officers discovered that a small percentage of captains were responsible for a disproportionate number of sinkings. The decision was soon made that American submarine crews would be self-reliant and resourceful men, culled from a roster of volunteers. They paid the highest price of any service in the war. Of 16,000 men who made war patrols, 3,500 died.

Kess saw the boats as "sinister, effective fighting machines. I found them intriguing." And he willingly assumed the risks. "I wanted to come back in one piece or not at all. I couldn't bear the thought of missing an arm or a leg." Fighting on a submarine, however, had a unique risk: the dreaded depth-charging. As enemy planes or destroyers—named for their purpose of submarine destruction—cruised overhead, they would use underwater sound to try and pinpoint the submerged boat. Then they would loose barrages of depth bombs. If the explosion came too close, the boat would wrench, torque, and vibrate as if it were being used as a giant, aquatic tuning fork. "It was terrifying. There was nowhere to go," just try to evade and hope the soundman above wasn't too good at his job. Kess carried his love of machinery and systems home with him: He became a building engineer after the war.

STAN KESS
MACHINIST'S MATE
U.S. Navy
1937–1945

In essence, it was a love of machinery and engineering systems that carried him into the submarines. Wiry and slight, he was quickly at home in the "sinister, effective fighting machines. I found them intriguing," especially after an acquaintance gave him a tour of one. It was also the all-or-nothing esprit and risks of the boats: "I wanted to come back all in one piece or not at all."

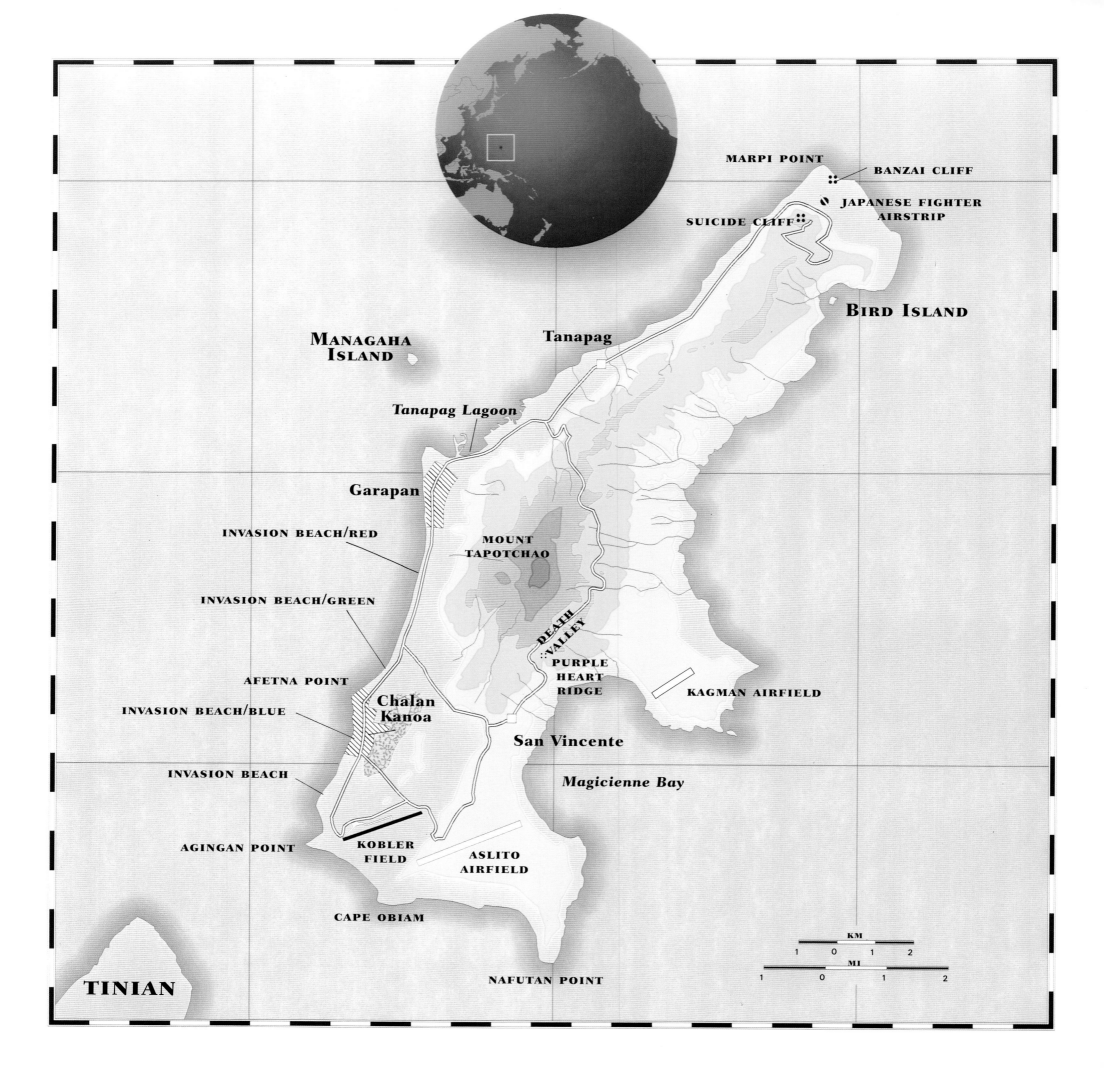

MARPI POINT

BANZAI CLIFF

JAPANESE FIGHTER
AIRSTRIP

SUICIDE CLIFF

BIRD ISLAND

MANAGAHA
ISLAND

Tanapag

Tanapag Lagoon

Garapan

INVASION BEACH/RED

MOUNT
TAPOTCHAO

INVASION BEACH/GREEN

DEATH
VALLEY

AFETNA POINT

PURPLE
HEART
RIDGE

KAGMAN AIRFIELD

INVASION BEACH/BLUE

Chalan
Kanoa

San Vincente

INVASION BEACH

Magicienne Bay

AGINGAN POINT

KOBLER
FIELD

ASLITO
AIRFIELD

CAPE OBIAM

TINIAN

NAFUTAN POINT

KM
1   0   1   2

MI
1   0   1   2

THE ISSUE: The first of the Pacific islands within B-29 range of Japan. THE TIMING: Approximately 20,000 marines landed nine days after D-Day in Europe. The 152,000 men assaulting the five Normandy Beaches sustained a casualty rate of about 8 percent the first day. One in ten men landing on Saipan was killed or wounded. THE FEUD: Two Generals Smith, "Howlin' Mad" of the marines—later criticized for a sharp tongue which proved counterproductive—and Ralph of the Army, relieved by his marine counterpart. THE AIR WAR: Japan lost its cadre of naval aviators in the "Great Marianas Turkey Shoot." THE CHARGE: More than 4,300 Japanese military men charged the beaches in the war's largest *banzai*. THE PLUNGE: An estimated 15,000 military and civilians, convinced surrender meant dishonor or torture at American hands, jumped from the island's two largest cliffs.

SHERMAN TANK
Abandoned 1944

EVERYTHING ABOUT THIS BATTLE was epic. The first troops landed just nine days after D-Day, meeting resistance as intractable as that at Omaha Beach.

A blood feud erupted between the marine commander, Gen. Holland "Howlin' Mad" Smith—with an opinion, usually pejorative, on anything—and the Army over the progress the Army's Twenty-seventh Division was making. The marine officer complained the Army was moving too slowly, exposing marine flanks to Japanese fire. The Army would counter that after Tarawa the marines had demonstrated their recklessness. "Howlin' Mad," defender of the Tarawa operation, was upbraided for starting an internecine feud in the face of enemy fire.

The Japanese Navy, meanwhile, was well aware of the stakes on Saipan. This was the first island within bomber range of Japan. Just four days after the first troops landed, imperial naval aviators went after the invasion force. More than 430 Japanese fighters and bombers attacked the American ships covering the troops ashore.

Officially it is the Battle of the Philippine Sea, but history records the day as the "Great Marianas Turkey Shoot." More than 330 of the Japanese pilots, many of them inexperienced, were "splashed" in the five-hour assault. The same day, the Silent Service joined in the victory and sent two Japanese carriers to the bottom.

◊ ◊ ◊

Governed by Japan under a League of Nations mandate, Saipan had a large civilian Japanese population. Convinced Americans would mistreat or dishonor them, an estimated 15,000 jumped from its cliffs. A French journalist, interned in Tokyo for the duration of the war, recalled that the battle for Saipan awakened the Japanese people that the tide of defeat was irreversible. News reports described the slow progress of the American advance.

◊ ◊ ◊

Their commander already a ritual suicide, the Japanese defenders mounted one of the war's most fearsome attacks: the *banzai* charge. The largest human wave of the war, more than 4,300 Japanese soldiers, sailors, and marines, considering themselves already doomed, broke for the beachheads in one night.

The result was carnage. They were soon joined by an estimated 15,000 Japanese military, civilians, and "dependents"—many of them children—convinced a plunge off the island's cliffs was preferable to their presumed fate at the Americans' hands. Some were driven at gunpoint.

In Japan, knowing all was lost, General Tojo resigned. American ground crews were already ashore.

One GI, expert in the electronics that would guide the B-29s over the trackless Pacific to Tokyo, was digging a latrine in the coral as the new bombers arrived. Their fighter escort, comprised of stalwart P-38s, buzzed the Saipan airfield. Exuberant pilots barrel-rolled their fighters into "wingovers."

The lead B-29, the *Dauntless Dottie,* piloted by Gen. Emmett "Rosie" O'Donnell, followed the example. He took his B-29, with a 141-foot wingspan, into its own wingover. The plane quivered but made the maneuver. Men in every quarter cheered. The war would be brought to the Japanese home islands.

SUICIDE CLIFF
Japanese Mass Suicide 1944

AMERICAN TANK
Disabled 1944

AMERICAN TANK TREAD
Thrown 1944

JAPANESE BUNKER
Surrendered 1944

AMERICAN BUNKER
Constructed 1944

JAPANESE AIR RAID SHELTER

Destroyed 1944

JAPANESE AIR RAID SHELTER
Constructed 1943

JAPANESE TRANSPORT
South of Saipan
Sunk 1944

To this day, Janney is uncertain why the Marine Corps deemed he should serve in the military police. A recent graduate of the University of Virginia, he had put down his course of study as "pre-law." Maybe somebody decided that was close enough.

With two brothers serving in the Army in Europe, Janney opted for his own path, becoming a marine officer. His assignment, with a headquarters company, was to collect prisoners, especially from among the large civilian population known to be on Saipan.

But his first assignment was infantry and he was in the first wave to assault the island. Janney recalls trying to cover the first dead marine he encountered. "I took my poncho off and covered him; then I tried to cover two or three more. But there's only so many ponchos you can find."

He remembers, too, one of the most dreadful *banzai* charges of the war, as Japanese defenders sought to drive the marines back to the sea. He remembers seeing row after row of enemy falling before American fire, as if some giant, dreadful scythe—truly a grim reaper—had cut a path to the beach.

Absorbed in the liberation of Western Europe, the world never fully turned its attention to the import of Saipan. The 20,000 marines who landed the first day and suffered casualties of 10 percent went home to private heralding.

ROBY JANNEY
OFFICER
U.S. Marine Corps
1942–1946

Janney chose his own route in life. With two brothers already serving in the Army in Europe, he became a marine officer. After the war, he accepted a ride with a friend and toured the countryside of his native Virginia. Their second stop was in Luray—home of the famous caverns—where he hung out his shingle and founded a family law firm.

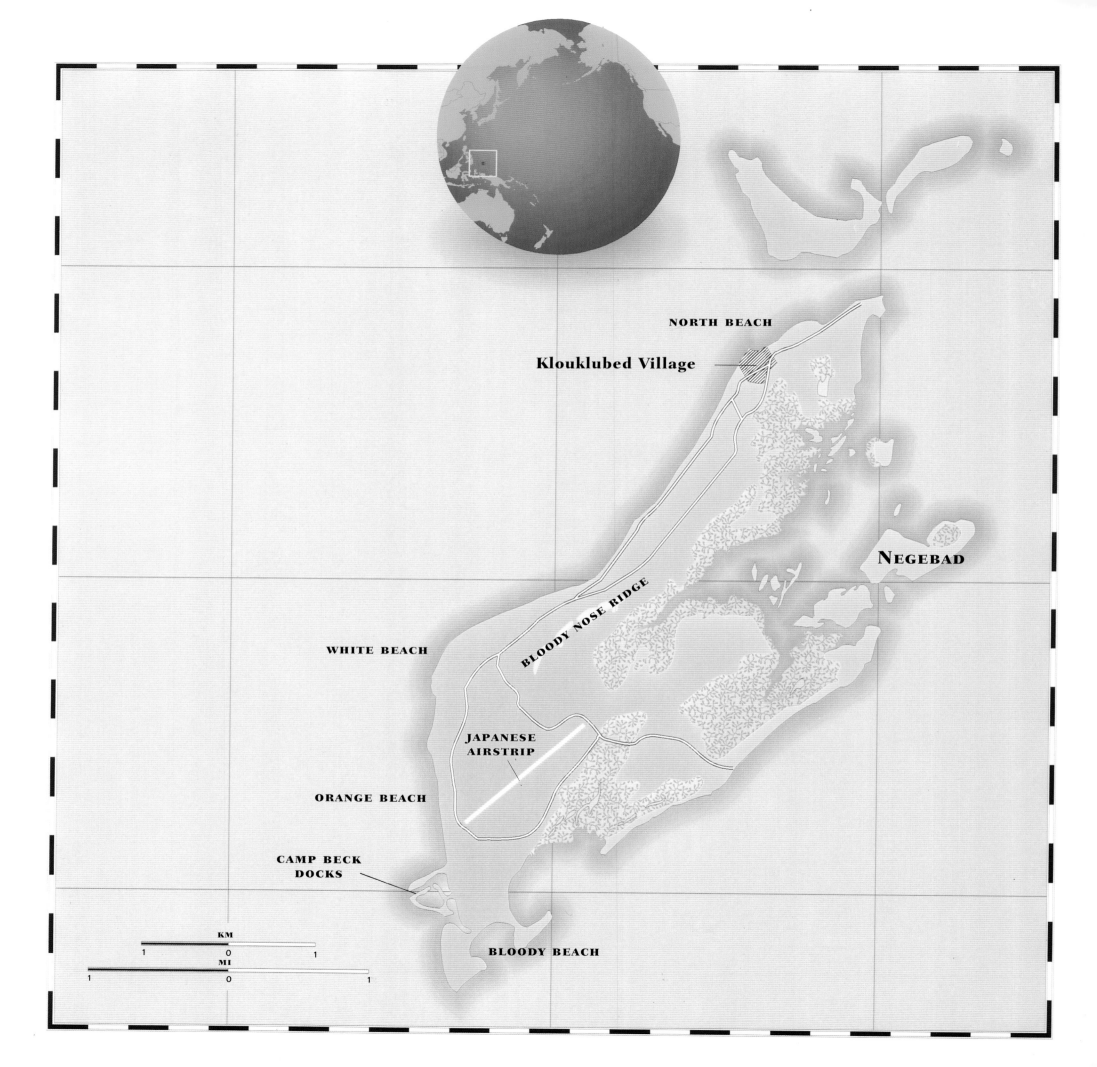

NORTH BEACH

Klouklubed Village

Negebad

BLOODY NOSE RIDGE

WHITE BEACH

JAPANESE AIRSTRIP

ORANGE BEACH

CAMP BECK DOCKS

KM
1   0   1

MI
1   0   1

BLOODY BEACH

THE ARGUMENT: Adm. Chester Nimitz and General MacArthur wanted the Palau chain taken, to cover the southern flank of the advance on the Philippines. Adm. "Bull" Halsey vehemently dissented. THE DETOUR: Peleliu, the main island of the Palaus, lies 500 miles off the Saipan-Iwo Jima-Okinawa-Tokyo track. THE DIVERSION: marines landed on September 15, 1944, while fighting raged in the Marianas. THE TERRAIN: Dry coral dust choked men and machines. It made cat holes for personal hygiene impossible. The island became a giant sewer. THE STRONGHOLD: Bloody Nose Ridge, a commanding citadel, which Japanese defenders gave up yard by yard. THE CASUALTIES: There were 8,000 Americans killed or wounded. The Japanese garrison of 10,000 and their 4,000 reinforcements fought virtually to the last man. 300 were taken prisoner. THE WASTE: Peleliu.

TENNYSON IMMORTALIZED THE SENSE of duty of the Light Brigade as it charged the Russian artillery at Balaklava: *Theirs not to reason why, / Theirs but to do and die.*

What Tennyson doesn't tell us is that it was a mistake. An officer pointed to the wrong cannon.

No poets immortalized Peleliu. Since the Civil War, massed weapons have bled the romance from battle. Poems, like "Flanders Field," serve only as elegy. The southernmost island in the Palau chain, Peleliu was invaded on the orders of Admiral Nimitz and General MacArthur—against the vehement advice of Admiral Halsey—on September 15, 1944, while troops on Saipan were still flushing the jungles as they laid down an airfield, as battles raged on Guam, and as Tinian was already being leveled in a triumph of aviation engineering. But the "brass hats" wanted to play it safe, which means sacrificing young men's lives for a chain of islands some 500 miles off the Saipan-Iwo Jima-Okinawa-Tokyo track.

Peleliu was where the Japanese debuted the "defense in depth" strategy: No longer would the first line of defense of an island be on the beaches. There would be no "first line" and no rear. These tough, determined adversaries would just stand, fight, and

Acknowledged as a detour on the track to Japan's door, Peleliu was thought to be lightly defended. Organized resistance lasted more than a month in one of the war's bloodiest battles.

die. Some predicted an easy fight. History reserves a special mockery—from the day-trippers sightseeing the carnage at Bull Run to the jaunty cockades of August 1914—for the forecasters of any "light" price in blood.

Marine advances on this would-be picnic were stopped cold, until Army reinforcements were forced on them. The last Japanese holdouts—in force—were demolished on November 27.

The victory was as Pyrrhic as the one at Tarawa. The Americans took more than 8,000 casualties destroying a Japanese garrison of about the same size.

Peleliu is at the southern end of a massive coral reef encompassing the entire Palau chain. To the Japanese, the islands afforded numerous advantages. For them, the Palaus were more than just another strategic archipelago, lying 1,000 miles west of Truk. The Palaus were their headquarters when they administered their League of Nations mandate over the Pacific (including Saipan). It was an important mining center; at the war's outset, it was a vital staging area for the thrust into the Dutch East Indies and their critical oil fields; at the war's demise, it was the new base to which the imperial fleet repaired after Allied air and submarine power denied it the use of Truk.

The Japanese honeycombed Peleliu with more than 500 caves.

AMERICAN LANDING CRAFT
Bloody Beach
Abandoned 1944

Repeatedly described as a "lobster claw"—no doubt the one used for crushing—it is a volcanic island, bereft of water, carpeted by dense, hot scrub. Much as at Guadalcanal, the airfield was dominated by a ridge. The native name was Umurbrogol. The marines, in another echo of the 'Canal, called it "Bloody Nose."

The Japanese fought with the tenacity and valor for which they were respected and hated. With the Japanese dug into their caves, the American advance was painfully slow once it reached the secured perimeter. They had to take each squad, cave by cave. In frustration, three rounds of flyers in Japanese were dropped over the island, offering safe conduct to the bearers. One soldier took the Americans up on the offer.

It took seven weeks to secure Peleliu. In an apocryphal incident, a wounded marine being evacuated from the beach was queried for souvenirs by a sailor. He rolled on his litter and patted his hindmost. "My ass, swabbie. I got out with my ass."

To the Japanese, every inch of Peleliu had to be bought at the highest price the Americans would pay. The casualty rate was almost 40 percent, the highest in any amphibious assault in American history. To the Japanese, Peleliu was vital.

But the Army's own final judgment is in the West Point history of the war: "Peleliu took its place beside the bloody fights of the Pacific War (Tarawa and Saipan) and the sanguinary American assault on Omaha Beach in Normandy. It did not, however, gain the strategic results which those other amphibious assaults achieved." Nor could it.

◊ ◊ ◊

Napoleon said an army travels on its stomach; commanders know disease kills the most warriors. Logistics and sanitation are crucial in warfare. The hard coral of Peleliu made it nearly impossible to dig cat holes for personal sanitation. The island became an open sewer.

◊ ◊ ◊

AMERICAN TANK
Disabled 1944

JAPANESE MILITARY HEADQUARTERS
Captured 1944

BLAST DOOR/JAPANESE MILITARY HEADQUARTERS

Destroyed 1944

BLOODY NOSE RIDGE
Assaulted 1944

AMERICAN TANK
Abandoned 1944

JAPANESE CAVE GUN

Captured 1944

A DOCTOR'S SON FROM a proud, educated family, "Sledgehammer," as he came to be known, eschewed officer training, preferring the iron-forged camaraderie of his marine rifle company. He served as a mortarman on Peleliu and Okinawa. Twice in the war, he heard a voice clearly telling him, "You will survive this war."

He emerged miraculously unscathed, and vowed to make something of his life. He became a biology professor.

Sledge also wrote a memoir. Called *With the Old Breed*, it recounts the incalculable in spare, ironic prose. Among many unadorned observations, one gives pause. Sledge and another gunner were detailed to a gun pit in which a marine had been killed the night before by a Japanese infiltrator:

[I saw] the white coral sides and bottom were spattered and smeared with the dark red blood of two comrades. . . . I had long since become used to the sight of blood, but the idea of sitting in that blood-stained gun pit was a bit too much for me. . . . As I looked at the stains on the coral, I recalled some of the eloquent phrases of politicians and newsmen about how "gallant" it is for a man to "shed his blood for his country" and "to give his life's blood as a sacrifice," and so on. The words seemed so ridiculous. Only the flies benefited.

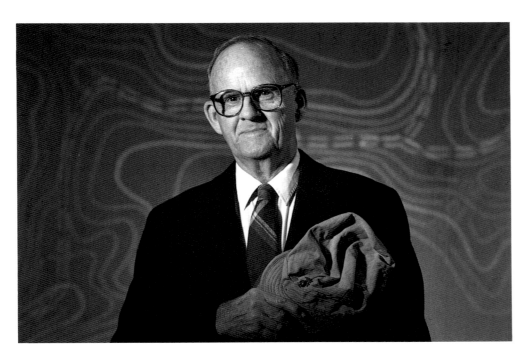

EUGENE B. SLEDGE
MORTARMAN/RIFLEMAN
U.S. Marine Corps
1943–1946

The marines offered Sledge a college education, in the V-12 program. It would have brought him an officer's commission. But half the class, anxious they would "miss" the war, deliberately flunked out. "If the program had been quicker," he recalled with an easy laugh, "why, we all would have been Rhodes scholars."

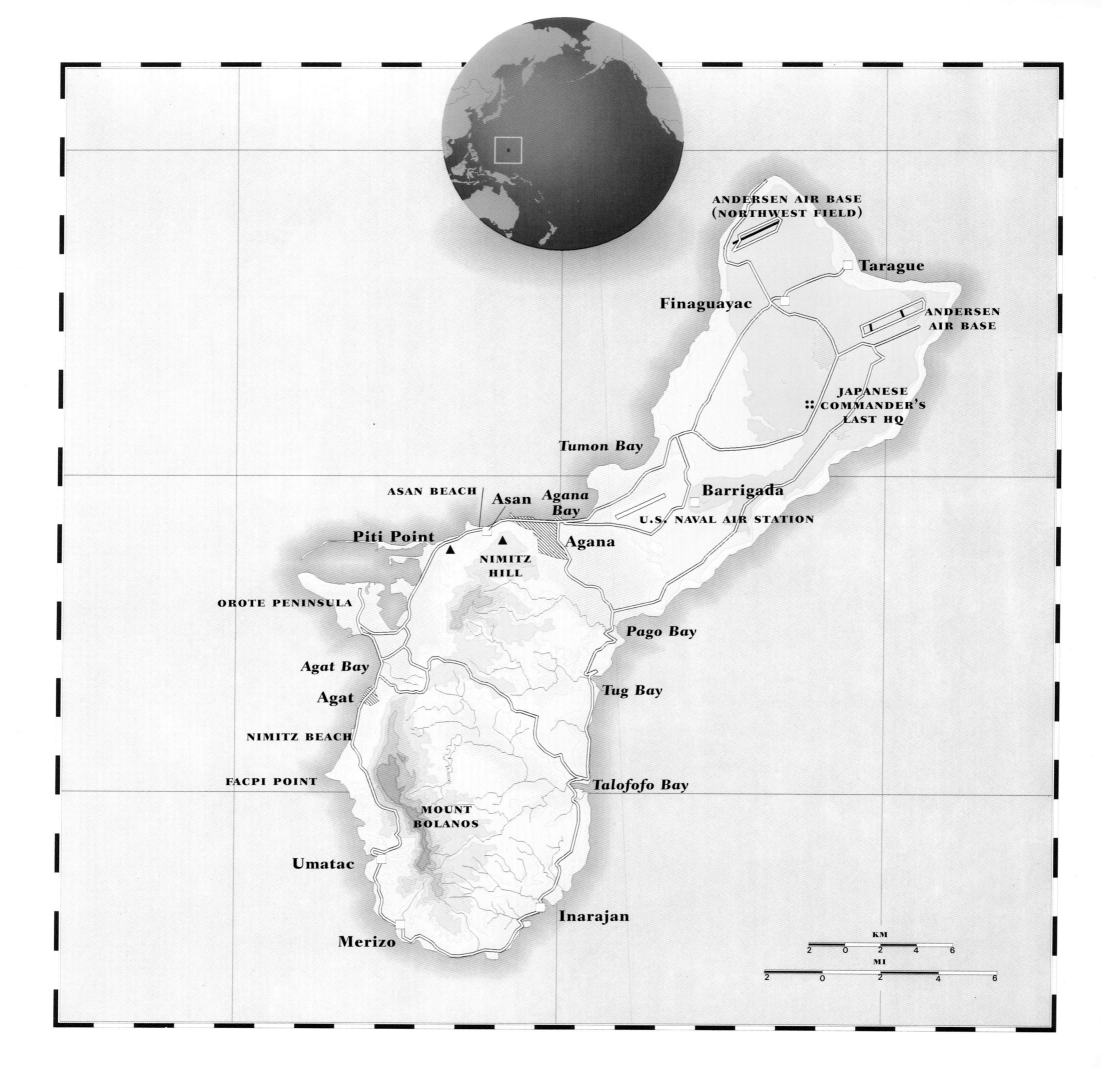

**ANDERSEN AIR BASE
(NORTHWEST FIELD)**

Tarague

Finaguayac

**ANDERSEN
AIR BASE**

**JAPANESE
COMMANDER'S
LAST HQ**

Tumon Bay

ASAN BEACH   Asan   *Agana
Bay*

Barrigada

Piti Point

U.S. NAVAL AIR STATION

Agana

**NIMITZ
HILL**

OROTE PENINSULA

Pago Bay

Agat Bay

Tug Bay

Agat

NIMITZ BEACH

FACPI POINT

Talofofo Bay

**MOUNT
BOLANOS**

Umatac

Inarajan

Merizo

KM

2   0   2   4   6

MI

2   0   2   4   6

THE RETURN: Seized from Spain in the Spanish-American War, Guam was prized as a coaling and water station in the mid-Pacific. Largest of the Marianas, it would be the first recovery of territory that was originally American. THE FIGHTING: A brief inferno, along lines at Asan Beach, Nimitz Hill, and Piti Point. THE DEFENDERS: Japanese efforts to repel the marines revolved around two offensives, one coolly planned, one bizarre. THE BREAKOUT: The garrison commander at Orote, knowing he was cut off, gathered his men for a desperate assault in the first week of the battle. Drunken cries allowed marine gunners to pinpoint the attackers and massacre them. Disciplined troops to the south found a weak point in the American lines and broke through to the beaches before their stand was cut down. THE CASUALTIES: The American force of 55,000 had casualties of 7,000, including 1,300 killed; of the Japanese garrison, estimated at 19,000, the Americans took less than 100 prisoners. THE HOLDOUTS: For decades afterward, solitary Japanese soldiers emerged sporadically from Guam's impenetrable jungles.

WHILE SAIPAN WAS THE BITTEREST battle of the Marianas and Tinian was prized for its air bases, Guam was the key island.

There were two reasons: One was psychological. America had held Guam for forty-three years—it was seized, like the Philippines, after the Spanish-American War. With one of the finest deepwater harbors in the Pacific, Guam had been a vital fuel and water station. Restoring it to American hands would be a strategic advance, but also a psychological one: the first time Americans had returned to soil wrested from them by the Japanese. The Guam landing was launched on July 21, 1944—a full three months before MacArthur would come ashore at Leyte.

The second reason was straightforward. Even today, Guam is a vital air base. Descendants of the B-29s based on Guam, the enormous B-52s, fly routine missions over Southeast Asia.

The campaign for Guam was fit for Hobbes, "nasty, brutish, and short." It marked the entry of such fighting

◊ ◊ ◊

Geography and psychology dictated the need to invade Guam. The Marianas had vital airfields. Guam has one of the best harbors in the South Pacific and was an American prize of the 1898 war.

◊ ◊ ◊

men's sobriquets as "Asan Beach" and "Nimitz Hill" into the lexicon of warfare. The American naval force included six battleships and five escort carriers. Following the virtual annihilation of the Japanese carrier fleet at the Battle of the Philippine Sea—otherwise known as "the Marianas Turkey Shoot"—the month before, the region was free from Japanese carrier-based planes, as well as most of the aircraft that had been based on Guam, which had also been destroyed. American carrier aircraft and naval barrages preceded the first landings at Asan and Agat. Eventually, over 50,000 troops with support from air and sea took almost three weeks to overcome the defenders.

The campaign also marked a kind of apex of the *banzai* charge. Two were mounted on the night of July 26. The commander of the Orote sector, knowing he was sealed off from relief and facing "defeat in detail," gathered his men in a mangrove swamp within sight of marine lines. Alcohol was broken out and the men were whipped into a fever. Every weapon at hand was seized—some marines reported

ASAN BEACH/NIMITZ HILL
Assaulted 1944

meeting enemy troops wielding baseball bats. The assault came after midnight. Decimating artillery barrages from American batteries swept the attacking troops before solitary survivors straggled back to what remained of the Japanese lines at Orote.

A calmer, though no less desperate, attack was mounted south of Orote, where disciplined Japanese troops found a weakness in American lines. Infiltrators broke through to the beaches and were within sight of American headquarters and a marine hospital. Every man became a rifleman—wounded were reported firing from their cots. By dawn, the Japanese dead numbered 3,500. The campaign for Guam cost American forces 7,000 casualties. Solitary Japanese holdouts

◊ ◊ ◊

Guam was the key to the Marianas, which were the key to bombing of the home islands of the Japanese Empire. But the island had an additional strategic value: Taking Guam put a knot in supply lines from Japan to Truk, 600 miles southeast of the American possession.

◊ ◊ ◊

would emerge periodically from Guam's dense jungles for decades after the war; the last survivor was discovered in the jungle in 1972.

Guam, however, became the nexus of American air operations in the Pacific. The commander of the Twentieth Air Force, Gen. Curtis E. LeMay—as strong a proponent of airpower as Billy Mitchell or Jimmy Doolittle—made his headquarters there. The forward headquarters of the Pacific fleet was moved to Guam, too, and American-style luxury followed the fleet.

Indeed, one general surveyed the plush accommodations available—even as fighting continued on Iwo Jima and raged on Okinawa—and was heard to remark, "This war could go on forever."

TREAD FROM SHERMAN TANK
Abandoned 1944

SHERMAN TANK
Disabled 1944

JAPANESE ARTILLERY
Piti Point
Disabled 1944

JAPANESE AIR RAID SHELTERS
Agana
Tunneled 1943

Though the *Enola Gay* departed on its fateful mission from Tinian and the first B-29 raids on the Japanese mainland left from Saipan, Guam was the nerve center of America's air war against the Chrysanthemum Empire. Holder of a doctorate in aeronautical engineering from the Massachusetts Institute of Technology, Doolittle was a true aviation pioneer: The first man to fly across the country in twenty-four hours, he then topped the achievement in twelve hours. Doolittle was also the first man to fly "blind," only with the aid of instruments he designed.

It was Doolittle who conceived the idea of launching B-25s—traditionally land-based bombers—off aircraft carriers to strike at Tokyo in April 1942. Launched from the deck of the carrier *Hornet,* sixteen bombers—Lt. Col. James H. Doolittle in the lead—rocked Tokyo. Though the raid did little damage, it had enormous impact on the course of the war.

Japanese forces were mystified by the planes' origin. As Doolittle's flight sped to friendly airfields in China, Japanese commanders reacted by seeking to extend their defensive perimeter in the Pacific. Japanese forces rashly attacked Midway on June 4—and were handed a crushing defeat that historians consider a turning point in the war.

On his return to the U.S., Doolittle was decorated with the Medal of Honor and asked to serve in Europe as commander of the celebrated Eighth Air Force.

Remaining an aviation pioneer, Doolittle filled a number of corporate capacities after the war, including work on the space program and as a director of several companies.

GEN. JAMES H. ("JIMMY") DOOLITTLE
AVIATOR
U.S. Army Air Corps
1917–1930/1940–1945

Perhaps no man symbolized the importance—moral and strategic—of American air forces than Jimmy Doolittle. Though his leadership of the April 1942 bombing raid on Tokyo made him a household name for a generation, Doolittle had, in fact, achieved a measure of fame before the war. He was one of the early aviation pioneers, a major innovator of instrument flying.

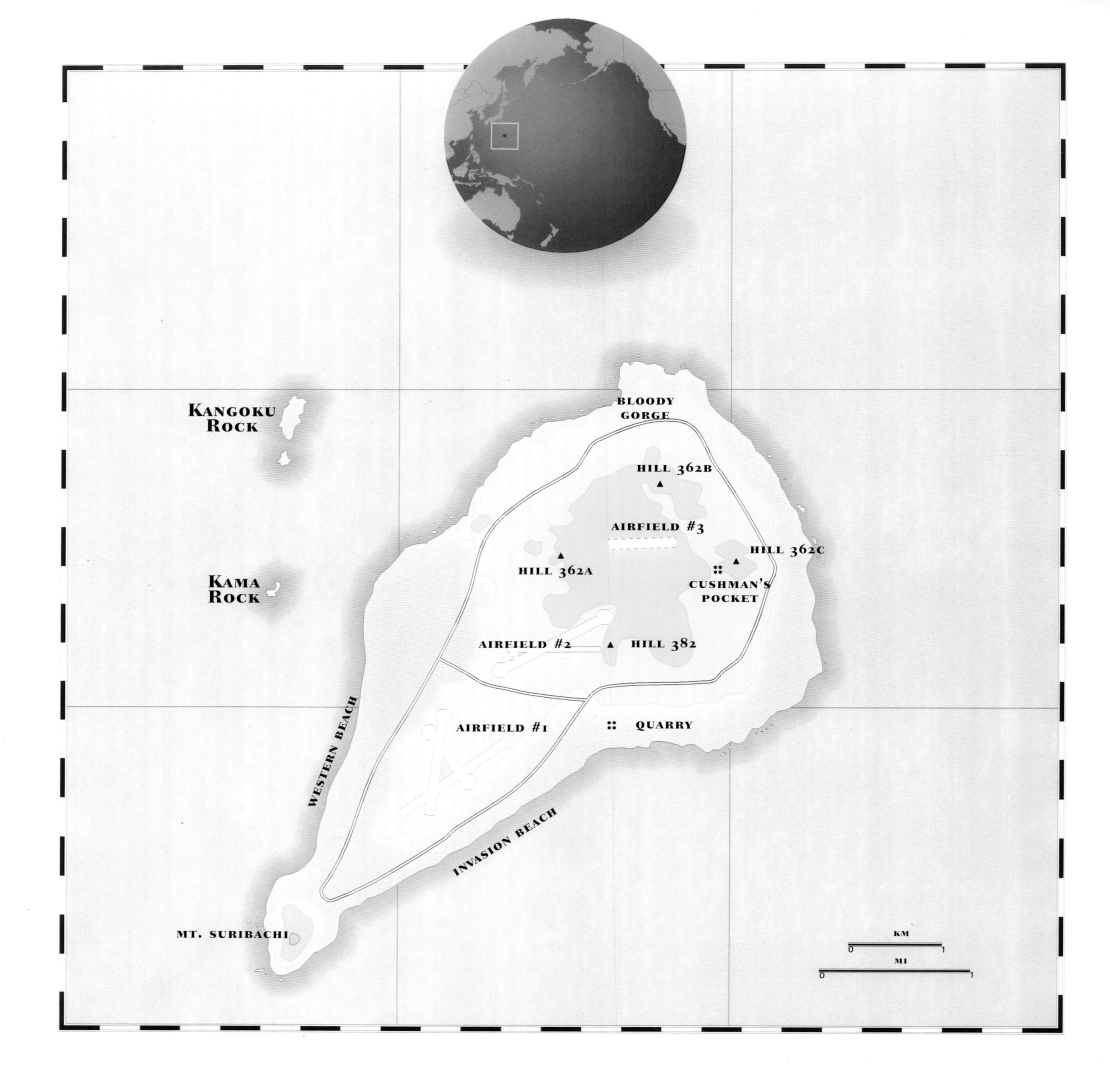

KANGOKU
ROCK

KAMA
ROCK

BLOODY
GORGE

HILL 362B
▲

AIRFIELD #3

HILL 362C
▲

HILL 362A
▲

CUSHMAN'S
POCKET

AIRFIELD #2   ▲ HILL 382

WESTERN BEACH

AIRFIELD #1   ⠰⠰ QUARRY

INVASION BEACH

MT. SURIBACHI

KM
0   1

MI
0   1

硫黄島

THE PHOTOGRAPH: Associated Press photographer Joe Rosenthal caught the raising of the flag on Mt. Suribachi, on the battle's second day, in February 1945. Three of the six men in the picture died on the island. THE DEFENDERS: Japanese engineers spent the autumn of 1944 preparing the near-impregnable emplacements of Iwo Jima. Observation posts and firing ports were dug, hardened, and concealed. The Japanese strategy was based on the premise that there would be no Japanese survivors, and that their fortifications would allow them to kill ten enemy soldiers for each man. THE FIRST DAY: marines landed on the black volcanic sand on February 19, 1945. One-fourth of them became casualties that day.

THE SPOILS: Iwo Jima's airstrip, needed as a way station for bombers en route to Tokyo from Saipan. The first damaged bomber landed in March, while fighting still raged. The island was also needed as a fighter base. THE COST: A total of 25,800 American casualties and 21,000 Japanese dead, on an island four miles long.

Iwo Jima, the "Sulfur Island," where the progeny of Cain wreaked havoc. Island of the infernally black sands. Emblazoned even in schoolboy memories by Joe Rosenthal's stirring photograph, "Iwo" was destined for bloodletting by more than the island-hopping strategy. Draw a straight line from Saipan to Tokyo—a dash of 1,500 miles—and it runs just east of Iwo at the halfway point.

Iwo was needed as a base for fighter planes, so they could cover the Marianas-based B-29s as they lumbered over Japan. Iwo was needed as a way station for damaged bombers. Iwo had to be secured to eliminate constant Japanese harassment of the air bases on Saipan, Tinian, and Guam.

All vital reasons for taking Iwo Jima. All desperate reasons for Japan to repulse the attackers with all the might of the empire. Iwo was part of Japan, home ground. For it to fall was unthinkable, as no foreign army had set foot on Japanese soil in 5,000 years. Knowing that it would eventually fall, the island's commander, General Kuribyashi had been told that inflicting heavy enough losses on the enemy might change Washington's mind about invading the homeland.

All the bitter lessons both sides had learned in eighteen months of amphibious warfare—since Tarawa in November 1943—were put to the test in a convulsive battle that began on February 19, 1945.

The largest armada of the war to date sailed to Iwo: 880 ships, over 100,000 marines, air and submarine support, all converging on an eight mile-square island. Prior to the invasion the island received the longest sustained aerial bombardment of the war. In the two days prior to the landing naval units poured approximately 22,000 shells into the Japanese defenses.

All to little, if any, avail. Aware that the invasion of Iwo Jima was inevitable, Japanese engineers spent the autumn of 1944 tunneling through and reinforcing the pear-shaped, four-mile-long island. The island was a virtual stone fortress. There were over 1,500 pillboxes and underground chambers connected by sixteen miles of tunnels. Mount Suribachi at its southern end, it's highest point, was thoroughly honeycombed galleries with gun emplacements up to five levels deep. General Kuribyashi's command center was a cement bunker with walls five feet thick and a ceiling ten feet deep, all under 75 feet of rock.

It was sinister and effective. There was virtually no location on the island that was not under cover by Japanese guns, the gunners themselves well-protected. The landing marines would not see the enemy for the majority of the invasion. There were no front lines.

◖ ◖ ◖

This is nothing less than Hell peeking into view. It was a battle both sides knew was coming—Iwo Jima is on the direct air route from Saipan to Tokyo. The carnage was diabolical.

◖ ◖ ◖

MT. SURIBACHI
Japanese citadel
Assaulted 1945

The first day alone, nearly 600 marines were killed and 1,800 wounded—about a fourth of the invasion force. The sand and volcanic ash slowed every movement in full view of Japanese gunners. It was a charnel house.

The flag-raising on Mt. Suribachi came after fourteen fruitless attempts to reach the summit. Historians debate whether it was the first flag-raising or the second.

The second? The third? The eighth? What does it matter? Precision is better served by recalling that half the six men in the picture died in the battle.

What the military believed they could accomplish in a week took thirty-six days. The ground had to be won inch by inch. Someone described the invasion as "throwing human flesh against reinforced concrete." The most effective weapons for an enemy that fought almost entirely underground were napalm, gasoline, flame throw-ers, and grenades. As the marines made their slow progress, the surrounding support ships were sporadically attacked by *kamikaze*. It was the bloodiest battle of the war to date, and a portent of what was ahead.

Many argue that, much as on Peleliu, men on both sides paid with their lives because of the preening of desk-bound egos. If Iwo Jima had been attacked in September 1944, immediately after the taking of the Marianas, the island would have still been largely undefended.

Instead, almost 6,900 marines died and more than 19,000 were wounded. The Japanese garrison of 21,000 was virtually annihilated, many of them sealed in their caves.

Surveying the carnage, the invasion commander, Admiral Nimitz, recorded the remark "Uncommon valor was a common virtue." Skeptics believe it was penned for him by a public relations officer.

◊ ◊ ◊

Some American military planners wanted to move against Iwo Jima as soon as the Marianas were secure, in the fall of 1944. But delays set in. Japanese engineers spent the season turning the island into one of history's mightiest fortresses.

◊ ◊ ◊

AMERICAN SHEET ANCHOR
Invasion Beach
Abandoned 1945

INVASION BEACH
Photographed from Mt. Suribachi
Assaulted 1945

JAPANESE CEMENT BOAT

Western beach

Constructed 1944

JAPANESE SHIP
Western beach
Beached 1945

JAPANESE BUNKER
North Iwo Jima
Destroyed 1945

SULFUR VENT
Eruption 1990

I HAD JUST GRADUATED high school, in January 1943, and went with my best friend to go sign up. The marines were full that day, so we went to the Navy. I thought the Army was dirty; I didn't want to slog through the mud."

In the Navy, he was sent to quartermasters' school (for navigation training) after he was found to be the only man in his unit with a high school diploma. He was also the only Jew, a situation that repeated itself later, when he was assigned to a "sub chaser"—small, speedy escorts that proved useful in a variety of roles.

Among his crewmates was a boatswain's mate from Ohio, a rabid anti-Semite. The bonding force of shared danger won out over bigotry, however. Marooned on a life raft, just off the invasion beach of Iwo Jima, they cemented a friendship.

Weinberg's sub chaser, outfitted with electronics instead of its usual array of depth charges and other ordnance, was a kind of traffic cop in the invasion. The 110-foot plywood-hulled craft could make twenty-five knots. Its shallow draft allowed it to maneuver within 100 to 150 yards of the beach. That's where it was, shepherding in landing craft, when the fantail of the sub chaser was blown off by friendly fire. As the craft settled by the stern, its Franklin life raft slid off into the water. For the next four hours, until they were picked up by a destroyer escort, Weinberg and his buddies were passive observers to one of the fiercest, greatest battles of the war. "Some guys were crying, some were praying. . . . You either find your faith in God and maybe dirty your pants, or become very detached. I watched the passing show."

STAN WEINBERG

NAVIGATOR

U.S. Navy

1943–1945

He rejected the Army because he hated the idea of having to slog through mud. His first choice was the marines—"We liked the uniform; we thought they looked sharp." But the local marines' recruiting station was already swamped that day. Weinberg later learned that the men of that contingent became part of the Fourth Marine Division, the unit decimated in the Tarawa invasion.

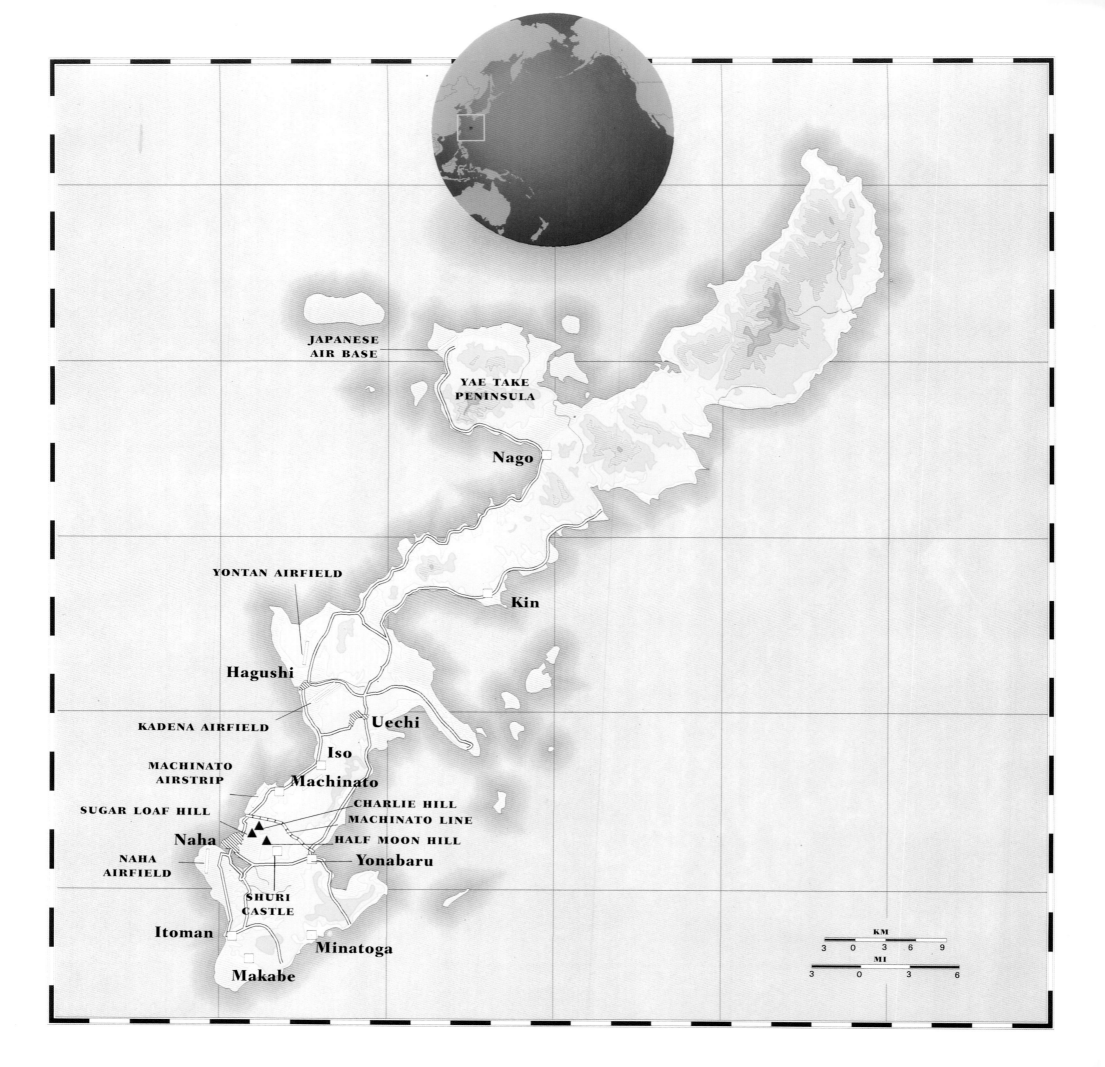

JAPANESE
AIR BASE

YAE TAKE
PENINSULA

Nago

YONTAN AIRFIELD

Kin

Hagushi

KADENA AIRFIELD

Uechi

Iso

MACHINATO
AIRSTRIP

Machinato

SUGAR LOAF HILL

CHARLIE HILL
MACHINATO LINE

Naha

HALF MOON HILL

NAHA
AIRFIELD

Yonabaru

SHURI
CASTLE

Itoman

Minatoga

Makabe

KM
3 0 3 6 9

MI
3 0 3 6

沖縄

THE SCALE: The largest island; the largest, most lethal battle. THE IRONY: The landing was on Easter Sunday, April Fool's Day, 1945. It was virtually unopposed in the northern two-thirds of the island. THE DEFENSE: The "Shuri" Line, a string of defensive positions anchored by the Shuri Castle, repulsed repeated assaults. THE SUICIDES: The ferocity of *kamikaze* attacks on American naval and Merchant Marine vessels became terrifying. THE CARNAGE: Over 12,250 marines killed and a further 36,000 wounded. Nearly 110,000 of the 117,000 Japanese troops were killed. An estimated one-third of the civilian population of 450,000 was killed or committed suicide.

IMAGINE A FUNNEL, into which swirls all the blood, ordnance, and accumulated lethal wisdom of more than three years of war. This, then, was Okinawa, a huge—by standards of the Pacific War—wasp-shaped island that was destined to shape the modern age.

Nothing was clear but that the largest, bloodiest battle of the war was dawning on April 1, 1945. It was Easter Sunday. This would be the last battle before an invasion of Japan's home islands. It was just 400 miles from the southernmost, Kyushu.

It was also, of course, April Fool's Day, a rubric which would be ruefully cited as the first 50,000 Americans landed, to challenge the 117,000 Japanese defenders. April Fool's Day all the more, because the landing—at cool forests and tilled, idyllic fields—was virtually unopposed.

Japanese forces, having long since abandoned the wrongheaded strategy of repelling invasions at the beaches, built three successive fortified lines across the bottom of the islands. Their orders were to hold these at all costs while aircraft from the Japanese mainland attacked the American support fleet.

It took six days of fierce fighting to get past the first Japanese line of defense. Withdrawing to the Shuri Line, with headquarters beneath Shuri Castle, they held domi-

◗ ◗ ◗

Knowing their Nazi allies had surrendered, the Japanese fought with the desperation of the cornered. Some historians say it was _kamikaze_ attacks off Okinawa that made Hiroshima inevitable.

◗ ◗ ◗

nating heights at Half-Moon Hill, Sugar Loaf, and "whimsically named" posts like "Gum Drop." Each had to be clawed through, sometimes slogged through as the rains came, turning slopes into intractable sheets of mud. It fouled weapons and tracks, turned morbid or wounded skin into running sores, made of the battlefield a mimicry of the World War I killing grounds.

Despite all the efforts of the massive American force, the Shuri Line held until May 21, when the Japanese commander withdrew to their last position in Naha. It was not until mid-June that the last position was overrun, and the remaining "clean up" took another two weeks.

Offshore, the Navy and Merchant Marine suffered under attack of, to that date, the most dreadful weapon of the war. _Kamikazes_ extracted a price of thirty-three ships destroyed and more than 160 damaged. An estimated 1,900 _kamikaze_ pilots sacrificed themselves to stem the invasion, along with an estimated 3,700 conventional sorties, most of whom were shot down as well. But the fleet was not driven away, and forward reconnaissance by submarines and radar ships allowed much of the attacking Japanese force to be dealt with before they reached the island. The Japanese sent their last great bat-

SUICIDE CLIFF
Japanese Mass Suicide 1945

tleship, the *Yamato,* along with the few remaining ships they could gather, towards the island. Carrier planes sank the 80,000 ton battleship halfway there.

Under unstinting artillery bombardment, seared by an incomprehensible weapon at sea, and appalled by the sight of the huge casualties among Okinawa's civilian population, many of the American troops broke down under the strain. There were 12,281 reported killed in the fight for Okinawa; another 14,000 were reported disabled by "neuro-psychiatric" disorders.

The disproportionate number of shell-shock cases was one of the smaller transitions occurring during the fight. By May 7, long before organized resistance had ended, Japan's ally, Nazi Germany, had surrendered.

The capitulation was received by a new President, Harry S. Truman. He came into office after the death of President Roosevelt on April 12.

Shortly after assuming office, Truman commented, "When they told me yesterday what had happened, I felt like the moon, the stars, and all the planets had fallen on me."

◊ ◊ ◊

There were an estimated 450,000 Okinawans on the island at the battle's outset. Of them, perhaps one-third died in the fighting. Some were sealed in caves and bunkers. Others were innocent victims of shellfire. Still more were cut down in the night by nervous soldiers preferring to "shoot first and ask questions later." Then there were those who preferred the cliffs to the torture they were told to expect from the Americans.

◊ ◊ ◊

The analogy was apt. Only hours earlier, Truman had been informed for the first time of the work of the Manhattan Project, and that it was close to successful development of the atomic bomb. The power of the atom would soon be put at his disposal.

Surveying the price for Okinawa, Truman did not object when his military planners told him the invasion of the home islands of Japan would cost Allied forces one million casualties. It seemed a reasonable estimate. With pockets of fighting continuing on Okinawa through the summer, Truman said later he was unhesitating in his decision.

JAPANESE CAVE ENTRANCE
Sealed 1945

JAPANESE NAVAL HEADQUARTERS
Captured 1945

PAVILION/SHURI CASTLE
Captured 1945

SUGAR LOAF HILL
Captured 1945

LAST COMMAND POST, JAPANESE 32ND ARMY
Captured 1945

RAMPART OF SHURI CASTLE
Assaulted 1945

THE IMPOSING, STERN-VISAGED figure of William J. Leyden belies the combat memories of a marine infantryman, veteran of the Peleliu and Okinawa campaigns. Leyden will smile benignly as he recalls that the rigors of training, desicating heat, and jungle combat had reduced him to 130 pounds. He remains bemused as he narrates film footage of the island campaigns. As wary soldiers, with flamethrowers, rifles, and satchel charges in hand, probe the aperture of a cave, Leyden points a cigarette at the scene and comments: "Even that's not the line," the front line of combat where he was stationed as a rifleman. Service "on the line" meant a plethora of horrors to recall. Moments like a Japanese soldier, emerging from a cave and hurling a grenade as he shouted, "Kill me, Marine, kill me" in flawless English.

Moments, too, when fate could be bewildering: As marines advanced they would inevitably bypass or overlook pockets of enemy troops. On Okinawa, one such pocket, a Japanese artillery crew, opened fire on Leyden's platoon from the rear. Four men in his foxhole were killed by a shell blast. Leyden was tossed into the air like chaff. Shrapnel killed two men on the lip of another foxhole scant yards away. He alone survived.

But he will be nearly moved to tears, viewing and reviewing footage of the body of a fellow marine being removed from a rocky ledge. "That's a touching scene." His sentiment bespeaks the camaraderie he knew in his rifle company. "We had guys from all over the country" pulling together in a cohesive unit. Though he would make careers for himself as a professional golfer and later as a car salesman, "they were the finest men I ever knew."

BILL LEYDEN
RIFLEMAN
U.S. Marine Corps
1943–1946

A battle-scarred veteran of the Peleliu and Okinawa campaigns, Leyden recalls his combat experience with equanimity. He can calmly recount the emergence of a Japanese from a cave, screaming in perfect English as he threw his last grenade. "There was another platoon about thirty yards to my left. If they hadn't heard it, I wouldn't have believed it."

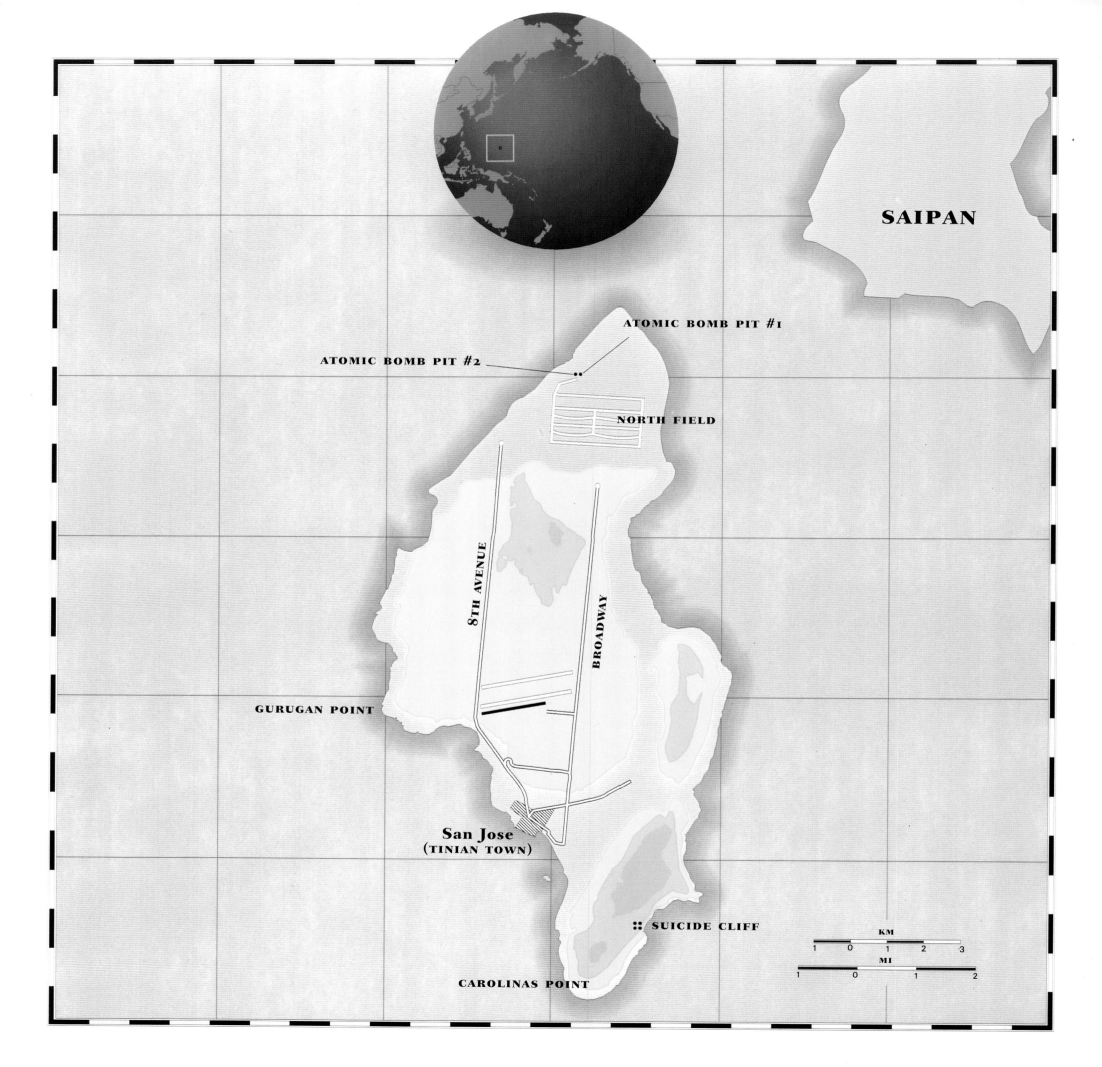

SAIPAN

ATOMIC BOMB PIT #1

ATOMIC BOMB PIT #2

NORTH FIELD

8TH AVENUE

BROADWAY

GURUGAN POINT

San Jose
(TINIAN TOWN)

:: SUICIDE CLIFF

KM
1 0 1 2 3

MI
1 0 1 2

CAROLINAS POINT

THE MISSIONS: The 509th Composite Group was based here, and it was from North Field that the *Enola Gay* and *Bock's Car* left on their missions to Hiroshima and Nagasaki. THE ISLAND: With a shape roughly resembling Manhattan, the island was turned into a giant air base, with thoroughfares named for Eighth Avenue and, of course, Broadway. THE FEINT: Tinian was called the "perfect invasion"—the only shore-to-shore operation—across the narrow Saipan Channel. This was the shortest route, but a massive fleet appearing off Tinian Town, to the south, bluffed Japanese defenders into believing they were covering the assault. THE ATROCITY: Shortly before the Americans landed, approximately 5,000 Korean slave laborers were bayoneted to death, their bodies incinerated in crematoria.

SOME HAVE CALLED Tinian the "perfect" invasion, if such a thing is possible in a battle with casualties. Lying just three and a half miles across a channel from Saipan, Tinian was invaded shortly after its slightly larger neighbor was declared secure. Artillery on Saipan supported what became the only "shore-to-shore" operation of the Pacific War.

It began with a feint, a show of force at Tinian Town (San Jose), on the southwestern end of the island. Because of the island's cliffs, the only suitable invasion site was at this end of the island and the Japanese expected the inevitable invasion here. They fortified these beaches, preparing to defend the three airfields completed on this comparatively flat island—a fourth was under way.

The Americans, however, took the advice of the Navy Construction Battalions—the famous "Can Do" Seabees—and quietly landed two regiments on the northern corner of the island, closer to Saipan. Within a week of the July 24 invasion, Tinian was under American control. The casualty count was 1,800—no cause for jubilation but a relief to veterans of the Saipan landings. The battle for Tinian also marked the debut of a weapon about which little can be said: napalm.

With Tinian "secure," the Seabees went to work. Because the island's shape resembled Manhattan, the roads they cut were dubbed for their New York namesakes. "Broadway" came to the South Pacific. The island was turned into a giant airdrome, with barracks, hangars, fuel depots,

◊ ◊ ◊

If Cape Canaveral is a hallowed place, what then is Tinian, where nuclear destruction took wing? For good or ill, Tinian, too, is hallowed. The atomic missions left from here. Much of the preparation of defenses was done by approximately 5,000 slave laborers shipped in from Korea. As the Americans approached, Japanese forces— no doubt anxious to save ammunition—bayoneted the Koreans to death. The bodies were disposed of in ovens familiar to witnesses of the Nazi horrors. A Korean monument to the massacre and its victims stands near the remaining crematoria.

◊ ◊ ◊

and round-the-clock takeoffs and landings. At one time, Tinian was the world's busiest airport, as well as its most lethal.

Soldiers on the island, however, knew that parts of North Field were off-limits to all but a select group of authorized personnel. The 509th was at work there. All some Seabees knew was that they had constructed two strange bomb pits. Whatever payload the 509th's bombers would carry, it was so heavy that the plane had to taxi over the pit for the cargo to be winched up into the bomb bays.

In late July, the heavy cruiser *Indianapolis* appeared off Tinian, delivered cargo, and departed. (Shortly after, steaming to Leyte, the cruiser was torpedoed. In one of the more scandalous incidents of the war, the *Indianapolis* was not immediately reported missing; of the 1,200 men aboard, 800 made it into the water, but four days of exposure and shark attacks took their toll. Only 316 were rescued.)

The delivery at Tinian, however, had been the critical mission of the doomed *Indianapolis*. The cargo was components of the atomic bombs.

At 2:47 A.M., August 6, 1945, the *Enola Gay* and her escorts lifted off from North Field. Perhaps never before in history could a craft's captain and crew have been more destined to fix a point in history.

Three days later, on August 9, the mission for Nagasaki, armed with the plutonium bomb, Fat Man, took off.

On August 15, Japan surrendered.

NORTH FIELD
World's Busiest Airport 1945

HEADQUARTERS OF AMERICAN 509TH BOMBARDMENT GROUP
North Field
Erected 1944

ATOMIC BOMB PIT #2
North Field
Nagasaki ("Fat Man") Bomb, Loaded August 8, 1945

RUNWAY #4
North Field
Enola Gay takeoff, 0247 hrs., August 6, 1945

GATE OF HEAVEN
Erected 1941

TIBBETS WAS THE PILOT of the *Enola Gay* (named for his mother), B-29 which dropped the bomb on Hiroshima, and commander of the 509th Bomb Group—a unit specially organized for the atomic missions. He achieved a reputation as a superior aviator early in the war, during missions in the casualty-strewn skies over Europe. Though his first bomber, a B-17 called *Butcher Shop*, saw its share of missions, he was also picked for such delicate missions as piloting Gens. Mark Clark and Dwight David Eisenhower to key rendezvous.

The missions of the 509th demanded more than mere competence from fliers. Meeting with J. Robert Oppenheimer, the scientific head of the Manhattan Project—the massive effort for development of the bomb—Tibbets was told that calculations showed the bomber delivering the bomb would have to be eight miles from the blast at the time of detonation. Tibbets's

solution was to develop a unique turn—by trial and error. Alone, he took a B-29 aloft and experimented repeatedly at 30,000 feet. Once he found the formula, all the other crews would use it: Over Hiroshima, the plane made a 159-degree turn to the right and began to climb at a 40-degree angle. His rate of climb was three degrees per second.

Controversy about the use of the atomic bomb continues to rage. Tibbets, however, adds an interesting point of view. He believes strongly that the missions of the 509th Bomb Group hastened the end of the war, a conviction strengthened during a visit by a delegation of young Japanese businessmen several years ago. They thanked him, Tibbets said. By shocking Japan's militarist leadership into surrender, Tibbets was told, the atomic bombs dropped on Hiroshima and Nagasaki actually saved their fathers from sacrificing themselves.

BRIGADIER GENERAL PAUL W. TIBBETS
PILOT
U.S. Army Air Corps–Army Air Force
1937–1966

Customarily, bombers are directly over their targets as their payloads explode. But the head of the Manhattan Project told Tibbets the plane would be annihilated if a traditional bombing run was attempted. He pushed the B-29 to the limits of its engineering to develop a radical new turn away from the blast. When the plane started to shake, he knew he could go no farther.

AUTHOR'S NOTE

W HY ARE YOU DOING THIS?" Very good question, one that certainly crossed my mind many times in the two years that it took to produce *War of Our Fathers* and the seven years since. Three shooting trips, six months overseas, nine visits to Japan, 120,000 air miles, 10,000 miles in automobiles . . . forty or fifty mosquito bites on my forearms in one memorable hour in a malarial swamp outside Madang, Papua New Guinea.

Why are you doing this?

Well, for one thing, so I'd have the opportunity to stand in that nasty little pond and get to see my first really intact World War II aircraft in its natural setting. That first plane was a Japanese light bomber, mostly just a silvery shell by 1990, situated in what appeared to be a wildly overgrown, limitless greenhouse.

It was a magical sight.

My father served briefly in the Pacific Theater in World War II, and it was through him that, as a child, I first became acquainted with some of the history of that war.

Like most servicemen and servicewomen, even those stationed overseas, my father did not participate in combat. He never fired a shot in anger, and was never sure that any were specifically aimed at him. His closest brushes with death were aviation mishaps that, while deadly serious when they happened, the passage of time and the great blessing of survival long ago turned into fond memories.

The Army Air Force was good to Allan Marin. He earned within it the rank of captain, was given the opportunity to further his education, both formal and informal, and at the end of the war experienced the great adventure of serving his country overseas as an officer in an army that had, effectively, conquered the world.

On August 30, 1945, he arrived at Atsugi Airbase outside Tokyo aboard the twenty-seventh American aircraft to land—six hours before General Douglas MacArthur walked down the ladder of his personal aircraft, *Bataan*. My father helped prepare for MacArthur's arrival, a job and working environment that I am reliably informed he found fascinating and, basically, enjoyable.

RICHARD MARIN
Peleliu
Praying for Sun 1990

CAPTAIN
ALLAN MARIN
U.S. Army Air Force
Okinawa 1945

That day he celebrated his birthday in Tokyo. He was thirty-three years old.

Like many other veterans, my father treasured the friendships that he formed during the war far more that any martial achievements. I can vividly remember visits from the three generals my father served: Maj. Gen. Lucas V. Beau, Maj. Gen. Victor E. Bertrandias, and Brig. Gen. Albert E. Boyd.

Boyd always made the most dramatic entrances. He was a renowned test pilot and always seemed to manage to hold jobs that provided him with his own aircraft. To a ten-year-old boy the sight of your father's friend flying into gray little Meigs Field on the Chicago lakefront—in his own aircraft—was pretty impressive.

This was in the 1960s, twenty years and more after the end of World War II. These men came to our family's home for one reason: to see Dad.

Only when I began to explore military history did the magnitude of the Pacific War begin to reveal itself.

The Greater East Asia Co-Prosperity Sphere, created by Japan, at one time encompassed one-fifth of the Earth. Their military was one of the toughest and most disciplined fighting forces in history. Elements of genius were exhibited by military leaders on both sides of the conflict: Halsey, Yamamoto, Stilwell, Doolittle, Yamashita, and America's most creative general of the twentieth century, Douglas MacArthur.

Some battles took place in locations that were so rugged as to almost defy description—the Owen Stanley Mountains in New Guinea were certainly one of the most surreal battlegrounds in military history.

In some places the space in which the forces were concentrated was microscopic: Betio, the island within the Tarawa Atoll where all the significant fighting took place, is half the size of Central Park in New York City. More than 8,000 combatants were killed or wounded on Betio in the space of one nightmarish week.

Some battlefields were both incredibly rugged and astonishingly tiny: Peleliu and Corregidor islands, in particular, stand out in this regard.

All counted, nearly 3,000,000 Americans served in the Pacific, with my father and his friends marching among them.

So here was the idea: I wanted to see what my father and his friends had seen, and I wanted to honor them with that vision. In recognition of the great gift of the support of my friends, I hope in some small way I have accomplished this mission.

In any undertaking of this scope the photographer becomes something of a passenger on the ship of his own creation. Certainly not, at many times, its captain. He is utterly dependent on countless individuals whose unpaid or underpaid contributions collectively make or break the project. There are many Samaritans I have met along this journey whom I am unable to properly credit here—you know who you are and I hope you know that you have my heartfelt thanks.

War of Our Fathers received early support from the Professional Photography Division of Eastman Kodak Company.

My deepest thanks are extended to Raymond DeMoulin for valuing these photographs—when they didn't exist anywhere but in my mind.

It is only through the vision, faith, and hard work of my publisher in Japan, Reimon Nishiwaki, editor in chief of TBS-Britannica, that the Japanese language first edition of *War of Our Fathers* came to be published in 1991. His support of this project and respect for its goals is deeply appreciated.

Both the first English language edition of *War of Our Fathers* and this second edition were made possible in a large part by John Kelly, as Publisher of Barnes & Noble Books, and now as principal of Book Creation, LLC. My gratitude to him for his appreciating the value of making these images available in America cannot be overstated, nor can my thanks for his crafting of the final text.

It is with great humility that I thank both Stephen E. Ambrose and Senator John McCain for, respectively, the beautiful fore-

word and afterword. *War of Our Fathers* could not have hoped for better, or more generous and gracious, contributors.

Dennis and David Barnett of The Barnett Group, the designers of *War of Our Fathers*, showed incredible patience and staying power during the two years the book was in production and in the nine years since. Their contributions are fundamental to the project in every way, and their judgment and sensibilities have been, and remain, essential to me.

I am forever indebted to my friend Akinori Itoh, proud son of the late Technical Sergeant Bansuke Itoh of the Imperial Japanese Army, for his essential assistance in bringing this book to publication in Japan—and indirectly in America. Without his steadfast support and constant counsel this book would never have existed in any language.

I thank Samuel K. Skinner, secretary of transportation and the President's chief of staff in the George Bush administration, for making it possible for me to stay at the U.S. Coast Guard LORAN station on Iwo Jima. His support made possible documentation of an island without which this project could never have been considered complete.

Within the Coast Guard I would like to thank Comm. J. J. Hathaway, Capt. James Shaw, and Lt. Jeffrey Ruvolo for their cooperation and patience.

I am indebted to Congressman John Porter of Illinois, for his help arranging for the Military Airlift Command to allow me on its flight to Iwo Jima.

Within the photographic community I would like to thank three old friends, Greg Heisler, Steve Krongard, and Harris Welles for encouraging me to attempt this project. My assistant, Joshua Sheridan, proved to be the professional that I've always know him to be in helping assemble the equipment required to execute the portraits, and assisting on those shots. Finally, Warren Motts, former chairman of the board of the Professional Photographers of America, brought his enthusiasm, generous assistance, and unique personal relationships to this enterprise.

Supervision of the black-and-while film processing and

reproduction printing was the work of Varouj Kokuzian, Senior Creative Genius, B&W, Gamma/Chicago. It is not possible for me to overstate his skills and sensitivity, and the contribution he has made, not only to this project, but to my craft over many years.

At the genesis of *War of Our Fathers* was William Manchester's remarkable and evocative memoir of the Pacific War, *Goodbye Darkness*. I thank the Professor for the inspiration that *Goodbye Darkness* provided, and for his many other important histories.

I also wish to thank Steven Speilberg for the great revelation of *Saving Private Ryan*, and the gift of the vast positive effect it has had on Americans' appreciation of the value and importance of memorializing the sacrifices of the World War II generation.

Overseas, logistics and information became everything. The kindness, knowledge, and generous help of strangers, now friends, made possible the *War of Our Fathers* photographs. On Guam: the outrageous Bob Couch and Al Maki, with whom many exquisite adventures were shared and many remarkable relics visited. In New Guinea: the immaculate Lt. Col. Michael Dennis, MBE, then Australian military attaché to Papua New Guinea, who provided many insights into the Australian viewpoint on the New Guinea campaign—as well as excellent, fatherly security advice; also, Michael Montgomery of Pacific Helicopters for the best helicopter charter ever and a very entertaining visit to the mining camp outside Wau. On New Britain: Bob and Rena Lane of the Kaivuna Hotel for their graciousness and assistance. On Guadalcanal: Ellison Kyere of the Solomon Islands Tourist Office for making my all-too-short stay productive and fun. On (and over) Peleliu: Bob Keys of Palau Paradise Air for great aerial photography flying. On (and under) Truk Lagoon: Gradvin Aisek of Blue Lagoon Dive Services for getting this (then) nondiver down and back up again safely—as well as for introducing me to the limitless majesty of the ocean. On Tinian: Elder Cory Reid and Elder José Jaime, missionaries of the Church of Jesus Christ of Latter Day Saints, for their companionship and tolerance of my cursing. On Saipan: the fabulous Jake Thornburg, artist and philosopher, for his assistance, climbing and caving skills, and his unique view of the underground world of the Japanese fighting man.

Finally, I would like to thank the twelve American veterans who graciously consented to be photographed for this book. It was an honor to have met each of you, and I apologize for taking so long to complete this mission.

Some of the more adventurous readers of this book may choose to visit these islands. All I can ask is that you not mar the magical quality of these sites with graffiti. I'm sure that "Tony/New Jersey/8-14-89" and "Bobby/Arkansas/3-12-88" were very proud that they had visited one of these battlefields, but it was disgusting to be reminded of it.

The battlefields of the Pacific are far more than mechanical graveyards—they are sacred ground upon which tens of thousands of Americans and Japanese made every possible sacrifice. It is essential to our humanity that we accord these physical reminders of their struggle with respect.

A note to those who plan to travel to these islands: I hope that you are not disappointed by your visit. Please understand that these photographs do not reflect what these relics "really" look like. These photographs bear little more relation to what's out there than my dream of a beach does to the beach itself.

RICHARD MARIN
Evanston, Illinois
March 30, 2001

AFTERWORD

MY GRANDFATHER WAS A NAVAL AVIATOR, my father a submariner. They saw each other for the last time on the bridge of the *USS Proteus* in Tokyo Bay a few hours after the Second World War had ended.

On the day of their reunion, my father and his crew had just brought a surrendered Japanese submarine into Tokyo Bay. My grandfather had just relinquished command of our renowned fast carrier task force in the Pacific, and had attended the signing of the Japanese surrender aboard the *USS Missouri* that morning. He would die at home days later. My father, inspired by his example, would go on to command all American forces in the Pacific in a later war.

My father and grandfather were my first heroes, and my understanding of World War II comes through my identification with their role in it. The same is true of many Americans whose forefathers fought our greatest war and secured a noble peace for us who followed.

War of Our Fathers captures with elegance and almost supernatural beauty the savage battlefields of the Pacific theater, in tribute to those who made the victory ours. In what seems today a near-mythical era of honorable men who lived and died for love of a cause they called glorious, our fathers and grandfathers left the farms, factories, and schools of America to wade, fly, sail, and storm into the swirling cauldron of war that was the Japanese-owned Western Pacific.

Their lives, and ours, were forever changed by their struggle. This book shows how grave was their sacrifice, and is a haunting memoir for men who once knew these atolls, reefs, and cliffs not as compelling photographs, but as impregnable and all-too-real fortresses to overcome at terrible cost.

Listen to the old men talk of these things, and re-live their stories. Old, humble men who, in the face of grave danger and unspeakable atrocity, brought light to half a world that had been plunged into darkness.

Go there with them through the pages of this book. Like me, you will emerge with an abiding appreciation for these present-day monuments to glory.

Look closely at the black beaches of Iwo Jima and see the blood of the Marines staining the sand. Squint at the cliffs on Saipan and witness thousands of civilians leap to their deaths rather than surrender. Peer into the jungle of Guam decades after the end of hostilities and see the lonely eyes of the Japanese soldier who is still fighting a lost war. Dive below the waves of Truk Lagoon and swim among its haunted depths, where a great navy lies dormant in memorial to the cruel ambitions of its masters. Look up at Mount Suribachi and know the glory of the Marines who raised the Stars and Stripes on its summit after one-quarter of their number fell on the first day of battle.

My grandfather, an aircraft operations commander

early in the Pacific War, witnessed first-hand the fierce Japanese bombing of Guadalcanal. One of the toughest men I have ever known, he became emotional, often crying, when he recalled the faces and spirit of Marines and pilots defending Henderson Field in those exhausting early weeks of the campaign.

He spoke of his young pilots who took a beating unequaled in the annals of war. He told one of his air commanders that the pilots he met there had resigned themselves to die for their country and had shaken his hand with the attitude of men taking a last farewell.

For the rest of the war, the loss of a single pilot would distress him terribly. I suspect every casualty report he read must have summoned up the faces of those fatalistic pilots on Guadalcanal who were ready to die at his command.

War of Our Fathers evokes the memories of veterans of the Pacific theater. The sublime beauty of the images it captures takes those of us who were not there into the world of our fathers who were. May we honor their sacrifice for as long as the waves wash over the reefs of Bloody Tarawa and the sun sets over the still heights of Mount Suribachi.

JOHN McCAIN
Phoenix, Arizona
February 23, 2001

ABOUT THE PORTRAIT SUBJECTS

To try and summarize the Pacific Theater in twelve visages is a daunting—and rapidly becoming impossible—task. We wish to say at the outset that we used something veterans will recognize as the "hey you" system. We simply asked everyone we knew to identify veterans they knew.

It is sometimes said that Americans have no sense of history. Let this project put the lie to that canard. We were gratified by the outpouring of contacts, suggestions, and offers of assistance.

In truth, out of perhaps 100 queries, we were rebuffed only twice. One refusal stands out: We wanted to memorialize the contribution of the Navajo code talkers, but less scrupulous authors preceded us and "burned the bridge."

Some veterans portrayed were close at hand. Some, such as General Tibbets or General Doolittle, were somewhat remote to us.

We hope we have selected a mix of services, regions, and contributions to the war effort. Some were of historic significance, some just "did their bit" and went home. To us, all were deserving of gratitude and recognition.

Right Motives give
Pinions to Thought
and Strength
and Freedom
to Speech
and Action

Allan Marshall Marin
1912-1999